THE
TRANSITION

★★★ PREPARING FOR FINANCIAL COMBAT ★★★

CPT(R) LARRY WALLACE JR., PH.D.
Disabled - Veteran / U.S. Army

COL(R) HEATH J. NIEMI
Combat Disabled - Veteran / U.S. Army

PREFACE

The Transition: Preparing for Financial Combat is about preparing transitioning service members psychologically for the next stage of their life after the military. This book approaches every facet of a transition with unique insight and helpful techniques to better mentally prepare and create the proper self-awareness to succeed and thrive within the civilian workplace. The better prepared a service member becomes through their transition, the greater the chances in achieving their desired lifestyle and goals. The Transition is truly invaluable because it assists our Nation's greatest asset, our service members.

While reading this book, think of the term *'The Transition'* as the catchphrase for your physical and mental state of change (from one aspect of life to another); whereas, *'Preparing for Financial Combat'* represents the psychological readiness required to succeed in obtaining your desired financial security. The support structures and systems accustomed to within the military will vary significantly once separated. Therefore, how you plan your transition along with the decisions made along the way, impact your post-military financial security.

The layout of this book encapsulates the process to successfully develop the self-awareness and psychological stamina required to meet and exceed your goals. Based on the structure of military publications and doctrine military personnel are familiar with, the table of contents, notes, appendixes, and hyperlinks (e-book only) enable easy access to desired information. A key benefit of this book is that it consolidates heavily dispersed information, simplifies difficult to comprehend programs, and serves as an alternative source for services.

CONTENTS

IN THE BEGINNING...TO SERVE

Congratulations! Whether you completed 20-plus years of military service or decided to exit the military early after years of serving our nation honorably—Thank You! We thank you for what you and your family have done and the sacrifices you've made for the greater good by volunteering to serve.

To serve is a calling. Serving is "a contribution to the welfare of others," according to the *Merriam-Webster Dictionary*. Having dutifully rendered your service to our nation, it is now time to focus on the next phase of life after the military, what we call *The Transition*. Financial security is commonly the largest concern for service members during this period because healthy finances ensure the welfare of you and your loved ones.

This book is specifically designed to provide a framework to mitigate the systemic challenges commonly encountered during this time after service. This book's purpose is to prepare you psychologically, and to assist as you navigate the nuances of Corporate America and the economic landscape you will likely encounter after your life in the military. *The Transition* offers useful recommendations and helpful hints to enhance your success as you enter this next phase of life.

THE DECISION POINT

Perhaps it is the culmination of time and rank (i.e., sergeant majors with 28 years or colonel with 30 years), reaching the 10-year mark and deciding not to go for the retirement carrot, or simply feeling it is the right time to take the next step; whatever the reason, now is the time to commit to your transition out of the military. It may be worth your while to consider a couple of items before making your final decision. Never make a transition decision rashly or emotionally.

First, take a few moments, go to the MyPay calculator, and forecast your retirement pay for several different courses of action. If you plan to depart before you are retirement eligible, compare the next promotion rank at three (3) years in grade (to receive full base pay at that rank) and ask yourself, "Could I make up the difference, outside of the military, for the remainder of my life having invested the right amount above and beyond my daily cost of living?" Even if you have found the golden goose egg of an opportunity or have landed a nice inheritance, you may find that the difference between a 05 with 20 years and 06 with 26 years, a CW4 with 20 years and CW5 with 25 years, or E8 with 20 years and E9 with 26 years is far more lucrative than imagined. Just maybe, staying in a few more years would be worth it. Certainly, your final decision should be made with all possibilities fully considered.

Additionally, you and your spouse need to find a good financial advisor who will produce a retirement plan that considers your current situation compared to your different retirement courses of action. For the future you want, do you have enough to retire on given forecasted inflationary rates, when you finally decide to stop working? How much will you need to provide for daycare, schooling, utilities, and amenities? And the culminating question: how much will you need to make at your next job in total compensation to reach your ultimate goals? The answers to these questions will frame and prioritize the factors you will consider when assessing job opportunities to achieve your goals.

THE REALITY

Although civilian communities receive well-educated, trained, and prepared citizens when separating service members join their communities as veterans, the ability of veterans to articulate self-worth as a monetary value is a distinct challenge. Regardless, veterans generate tremendous opportunities for success in their communities and for themselves.

Under the redesigned Department of Defense Transition Assistance Program (DoDTAP), the goal upon separation is career readiness for job employment, business ownership, technical training, and/or higher learning. Once TAP is completed, you should be prepared to offset unfamiliar labor market costs, adjust to modified military benefits, and meet general expectations to align your military skills with what the civilian workforce desires.

However, the notion that the DoDTAP alone can fully prepare you for the transition is a fallacy. The DoDTAP's sole purpose is providing information, tools, and general training to ensure service members and their spouses are prepared via "awareness" for the next step in civilian life. Quite often the DoDTAP is frowned upon given its design, yet it accomplishes its purpose. It is helpful to keep in mind that the military is a service authorized to use deadly force to support the interests of our nation and all its citizens. Therefore, the military and its leaders are focused on ensuring combat readiness through realistic training. Regardless of how much attention and support may be desired to enhance the transition for those who have served, resources remain prioritized to meet the top priority of the military, which is to ensure readiness for the defense of the nation.

Understanding the DoDTAP's framework and limitations, we can see how resources like this book and other products and services are needed. To summarize a statement by Michael Sarraille, founder of VETTED, we shouldn't expect TAP to transition us back into civilians; rather, we need Corporate America to assist the transition into Corporate America. Why? Because asking the military to transition veterans into civilians is like asking Corporate America to turn civilians into service members. When you want to make a soldier, you send them to basic training, a ranger to ranger school, etc. Therefore, a successful transition into a productive civilian depends upon training and assistance from Corporate America and other aligned resources such as *The Transition: Preparing for Financial Combat.*

Although this book is crafted for those in and near retirement eligibility, it is fashioned in a manner to also prepare, equip, and assist those interested in joining the military, new to the military, or who have been serving in the military for any amount of time; to include their loved ones and any others interested in and/or supporting those from the military.

EXIT PATHWAYS

Regardless of how your time in the military concludes, you may be provided some monetary compensation. Depending on which exit path you are eligible for and choose, you will receive either no compensation, short-term, or long-term financial support. There are three (3) basic exit pathways that hold a few programs within themselves. For example, *retirement* offers five (5) different long-term programs. *Involuntary separation* offers two (2) short-term programs, and *voluntary separation* may now include the thrift savings plan.

Note: Information for this section is drawn primarily from the Finance Management Policy, Military Pay Policy for Retired Pay.

Retirement.

Congratulations on achieving 20 or more years of honorable and distinguished service, which by law entitles you to either the *blended* or *legacy* retirement system, depending on your dates of service and opt-in selections. (You can read more about the systems in *Appendixes Q* and *R*.) The five types of retirement programs provided by the military are *early, regular, reserve, temporary disabled*, and *permanently disabled*.

2012–2025 Temporary Early Retirement Authority (TERA).

This program is only available to those deemed eligible by their branch of service (e.g., Army, Navy, Air Force, Marines, etc.) and who possess a minimum of 15 active years of service but not 20 years.

Regular Retirement.

This program is reserved for those that complete a minimum of 20 active years of service. (To learn more about the various compensation plans within this program, see *Appendix R*).

Reservist Retirement.

Reserve retirement is sometimes called a non-regular retirement for members who accumulated 20 or more years of qualifying service and reached age 60. However, any member of the Ready Reserve who is recalled to active duty or, in response to a national emergency, is called to certain active service after January 28, 2008, shall have the age 60 requirement reduced by 3 months for each cumulative period of 90 days so performed in any fiscal year after that date. There are two non-disability retirement plans currently in effect for reserve qualified retirees which are Final Pay plan (e.g., last day for highest grade satisfactorily held during service) and High-36 Month Average plan. There is no REDUX retirement plan available under non-regular (reserve) retirement. Similar to a regular retirement, the basic formula is Retired Pay Base X Multiplier %.

Note: Members must request retired pay from the military department last served because payment is not made until requested.

Years of Service. There are 3 categories for determining years of creditable service that have applicability to the computation of reserve (non-regular) retired pay.

Years of Service for Retirement Entitlement. This category of years of service includes each one-year period in which the person has been credited with at least 50 points (1 point for each day of active service, 1 point for each attendance at a drill period, 1 point for each day of performing funeral honors duty, and 15 points for each year of membership in a reserve component).

Years of Service for Pay Base. This category of years of service includes all periods of active service and all periods of Reserve or National Guard service counted day for day. A unique feature of Reserve retirement is that the pay base is determined as though the reserve member were serving on active duty immediately prior to retirement, thus the years of service continue to accumulate even after the member has entered the retired reserve and continue until they actually begin receiving such pay (usually age 60).

Years of Service for Retired Pay Percentage Multiple. This category of years of service includes all periods of active service (counted as one point for each day) plus all points earned through qualifying reserve duty, not exceeding annual limits, divided by 360.

Temporary Disability Retired List (TDRL).

For this program, your service Secretary must determine you unfit to perform your duties with respect to grade, rank, or rating because of a physical disability qualifying you for disability retirement. However, the disability identified is not deemed stable. Thus, the maximum number of years you are provided compensation on the TDRL is five (5), unless your Secretary determines your disability warrants an upgrade to the permanently disabled retirement list before then.

Note: You must complete a physical examination every 18 months to identify any changes regarding your rated disability. Compensation for your rated disability will terminate if you fail to conduct these exams or if your disability rating drops below 30%.

Permanent Disability Retired List (PDRL).

This program is for members with a disability identified as stable and granted at least a 30% disability rating. If you possess a permanent rating under 30%, you are eligible for disability severance pay instead.

Specialty Rank & Duty Assignments.

If an enlisted person retires within three (3) years of reduction in grade, retired pay will be based on final basic pay versus their high 36-month average. However, any promotion that occurs subsequently to a retirement will initiate a pay re-computation. Special basic pay is authorized for anyone retiring in the grade of O1E, O2E, or O3E with more than 4 years of active duty service. View pay rates at http://www.militarypay.com/MilitaryPayCharts.php. Joint Chiefs of Staff, Chiefs of Service, Commanders of Combatant Commands, and the most Senior Enlisted Service Advisors are authorized to retire with pay equal to the highest basic pay rate for that specific position.

Additionally, any retired enlisted member serving at least 20 years of active service or disability may be entitled to an additional 10% for extraordinary heroism acts, if authorized. For general or flag officers, retirement pay is as follows unless they served less than three (3) years in rank without a waiver. If a waiver is received, pay will be based on the computed time in grade.

Note: Retirement pay will fluctuate based on inflationary raises and other changes incurred by legislation.

0-9	Over 26-years of service:	$9,528.00
0-10	Over 16-years of service:	$9,528.00
0-10	Over 18-years of service:	$9,528.00
0-10	Over 20-years of service:	$10,167.00
0-10	Over 22-years of service:	$10,167.00
0-10	Over 24-years of service:	$10,167.00
0-10	Over 26-years of service:	$10,491.60

<u>Dual Benefits.</u>

If you're eligible to receive pay for both your active years of service and a disability rating from the US Department of Veterans Affairs (VA), you are barred from receiving concurrent payments of both retired pay and the VA benefit unless you waive your retired pay equal to the VA benefit awarded. However, you may qualify to receive your retired pay and VA benefit in full under the Concurrent Retirement and Disability Pay (CRDP) program.

<u>Financial Hardship.</u>

If your retired pay is subject to recoupment, you may, at any time, request a review regarding the amount recouped based upon verifiable circumstances such as disability, divorce, or an illness imposing undue hardship on you and your loved ones. If you desire a review, it must claim that your current rate of recoupment resulted in an undue financial hardship and provide the necessary supporting documentation.

Note: Your retired pay is also dependent upon your US citizenship. Additionally, a retiree may serve up to two (2) years in an active reserve or recalled status and receive compensation re-computation. However, if you elect to receive compensation for any training conducted, you must waive one (1) day of retired pay for each day of reserve training performed.

Involuntary Separation.

If involuntary separated, you are authorized a lump-sum payment due to being retired pay ineligible.

Disability Severance Pay (DSP).

This one-time payment is a program for individuals with a minor physical disability. Although there is no minimum amount of time in service required, the minimum number of years for computation purposes is six (6) for a line of duty at a combat zone designated line location or three (3) years for any other instance. The DSP is not available to individuals at 19 years of service.

Reserve Special Separation Pay (RSSP).

This one-time payment is a program for Reservists who have completed at least 20 years of service and are not 60 years in age.

Note: RSSP payments are not subject to retired pay recoupment. However, prepare for monthly deductions to occur if you receive separation pay and later qualify for retired pay. Additionally, prepare for your separation pay to be equally less than any eligible disability compensation received unless your disability compensation is received after your separation pay.

Voluntary Separation.

If continuing to serve is an option, it is recommended that you review the base pay for your next rank and assess the professional timeline required to obtain and retain that rank. Next, there are three (3) important questions to ponder: (a) is the monetary increase easily obtainable outside of the military, (b) is the additional time owed bearable, and (c) is obtaining that next higher rank highly feasible.

Regardless of how financially secure you may be; it is always important to make a well-informed decision before embarking upon the transition. The retired pay, separation pay, and disability compensation are perks for your service and should never be factored into your post-military livelihood unless absolutely necessary.

If the transition still looks like the optimal choice, seek a financial advisor to identify exactly what you must save to meet your immediate, short-term, and long-term goals regardless of how long it may take to start your post-military career.

Note: Ensure to forecast for inflation rates and compare all your courses of action to select the most beneficial option for your future. Moreover, disregard in your planning process the GI Bill benefits and potential tuition exemption given your planned residence to ensure you are fully capable of supporting any family education and training endeavors.

SELF-BRANDING

Who am I, and what am I, without the military? These are logical questions you may be asking yourself. You would not be the first, nor will you be the last. Until military counseling and evaluations more closely align with the quantifiable data sought by Corporate America, the road to articulating your capabilities will remain difficult.

What truly separates you from another with similar roles, levels of responsibilities, and training is how and why you did the things you did, with values illustrating the impact. Too often, service members and quite a few support groups extract evaluation comments without a true frame of reference to translate the full value in terms that Corporate America can understand. Comments like top 5%, among the best, promote now, etc., can possess different meanings based on the composition of the population. For example, being among the top 5% in a conventional organization versus a special operations force may indicate a significantly different level of operational experience.

Although unorthodox in the military, translating and communicating your personal worth is crucial for post-military transitioning. Thus, you must highlight the **ME** in team and the **I** in win. The benefit in telling a story of success or experience is when you clearly articulate your *actions*, their *benefit*, and impactful *result* (e.g., your ABC's). Quantification is key when promoting yourself; therefore, if you can't measure it, don't mention it. Corporate America is a world about decreasing expenses and increasing profits, so always ensure your discussions and materials highlight what's valuable to the hiring managers.

Note: Although the rank you obtained, awards received, and organizations you served in the military may mean the world to you, they may mean nothing to Corporate America, depending on the industry, company, and individuals you engage with. Therefore, know when and where to emphasize your rank, medals, and unique organizations.

RESUMES

A resume is a non-negotiable requirement for job searching. It is the quickest way an employer evaluates your experience, accomplishments, skill sets, academics, and attractive outliers (i.e., top-secret clearance). Therefore, put in the requisite amount of time to write up your past history, consider the importance of every word utilized, and precisely edit your resume for your desired industry, company, and job description. Heed to the importance of a resume when job hunting.

Resume Formats.

The number of formats to choose from—four (4)—comes from the tried-and-true standards. There is the CV (or Curriculum Vitae), which is a lengthy outline of every past job and work experience. Therefore, you may want to consider creating the CV first, then select your most relevant experiences, traits, and skills to create your two-page resume. Most companies and employment opportunities require a two-page (max) resume; however, Wall Street requires a one-page resume, which is not an easy feat. For federal jobs, USAJobs requires a government resume that is quite long—several pages. Of course, there are flavor-of-the-month formats as well, so investigate which format is preferred by your targeted company. Nevertheless, Signs of a Great Résumé: Veterans Edition: How to Write a Résumé that Speaks for Itself by Scott Vedder is a must have to start you off in the right direction.

Acronyms.

To civilians, the military's vernacular is pure jargon. Thus, it is important to translate your daily operating life into something they can easily understand—both in terms of what you send in writing and when you talk in person. For example, be cognizant about using MDMP, SITREP, FYSA, Roger that, Command Team, S3/A3/G3, etc., without relating and translating how those terms fulfill the job you are interviewing for. The following are a few recommendations to assist with this mental transition:

1. Stay away from acronyms when job searching because different audiences may think they mean something else.

2. Give a corresponding civilian job title with your military duty description (i.e., Director of Operations/S3 Operations Officer).

3. Ensure you translate everything for non-Department of Defense (DoD) opportunities and focus on just acronyms for those within the DoD. Most individuals within the DoD have a keen understanding of military duty descriptions and organizational structure.

4. Based on job description requirements, correspond experiences and accomplishments to meet desired traits for that particular job.

5. Always use quantitative and/or qualitative descriptors versus the military's more flowery language.

6. Choose words carefully. Most companies operate resume software programs designed to filter for applicants that best fit the job description. Therefore, use the job description itself when tailoring your resume. For example, most defense software filters look for the word *Pentagon* if applying for a certain opportunity like business development and drone companies for experience with drones.

For a frame of reference, you can use Glassdoor, Indeed, and other similar online resources to view sanitized, industry-specific resumes as well as company-specific information such as average pay range for a position, employee satisfaction, etc.

Master Resume or Curriculum Vitae (CV).

Unlike any other resume, the *master resume or CV* is a comprehensive document primarily utilized within academic circles and the medical industry because it elaborates on education, publications, and other various achievements. A CV is primarily used by master's and doctorate degree-holders applying for teaching or research positions at a college, university, or research institution. The *CV* is also used by graduate school personnel applying for grants, fellowships, etc. Unlike a *Wall Street 1-page resume* or *bio-resume*, the length of a *CV* is solely based on the individual's level of experience and length of accomplishments. New accomplishments are just added to the existing *CV* versus tailoring it for a job.

As you write your experiences down, be thoughtful in your words by ensuring every statement is quantified. The goal is to expose your common areas of expertise that are not specifically tied to pay scale (e.g., officer, warrant, enlisted), pay grade (e.g., lieutenant colonel, chief warrant officer four, sergeant major), and maybe even your specialized profession (e.g., aviation, human resources), depending on your areas of interest. If you already know and can clearly articulate your skill set to nonveteran leaders within your desired industry, great!

Nevertheless, it is recommended that you start with a master resume to quantifiably confirm what you know, to validate what you think you know, and to realize things you didn't know, to enhance messaging. It is meant to be a consolidation of all things you (i.e., professional, extra-curricular, etc.). Expect it to be as long as the experiences you possess and as comprehensive as your mind can remember the facts that only deal with you (i.e., led, managed, supported, provided input, etc.). List every position served, award received (e.g., coin, certificate, etc.), training program attended, and account for every hour of work rendered in support of self and others. Also identify your security clearance level.

Acronyms.

Keep in mind only 0.4% of the nation is a service member, with 14.6% as veterans. With 80% of the US population having never served, stay away from acronyms even if you believe them to be common.

Administrative Information.

When filling out your resume, consider how you will incorporate the following. Your basic information (e.g., name, phone number, email address, location) is provided within the header of the first page. If you decide not to use your official name, make sure what's listed is professional and includes your email address. To ensure callbacks for jobs in locations of interest, say "willing to locate," list up to three locations, or say "not willing to move" if that is the case for you. Also include your current location in case the company reviewing your information is not looking for someone who must relocate.

Depending on the amount of work experience you possess, inserting your education followed by work experience may be most beneficial.

Placement of your education and certifications is both a matter of preference and what your desired industry and company may prefer. Most inexperienced applicants highlight education first, then experience; while more experienced applicants place experience first, followed by education. Additionally, highlight any distinguishable academic achievements such as cum laude, 3.7 GPA or higher, honor society membership, etc.

Note: If you have multiple pages for a resume, ensure your name and page number are on the subsequent pages to mitigate separation or prevent them from getting out of order.

The Unit.

Labeling.

List the actual unit you served with because you never know who is looking at your resume. The recruiter or hiring manager might be military affiliated with knowledge of your unit or a nonveteran with friends they can inquire with. When possible, identify the type of unit (e.g., Task Force, Expeditionary, Special Operations, *USS Arizona*, etc.) as each additional bit of information subtly announces a level of professionalism, technical skill, and grit typically possessed.

Location.

List the state if stateside and country if overseas to highlight your worldly work experience requiring honed cultural sensitivity, inclusion, and diversity. Subtly, your duty locations (accompanying your bulleted accomplishments) can highlight the ability to excel regardless of the culture.

Descriptor.

Your first bullet should always enable the reader to relate your organization to a corporate business of similar scope and size. Therefore, list the total number of personnel assigned and supported; the hard (i.e., equipment) and soft (i.e., human capital) monetary asset value commanded; capital and annual operating budget; and its level of influence (i.e., Fortune 1000, 500, 100, etc.) to frame the organization's scope and size to something relatable.

Duty Description.

Title.

Base your personal descriptor on the exact roles and responsibilities you served as they relate to the industry and company you desire. For example, a company commander's role and responsibilities are equivalent to a chief executive officer (CEO), by definition, given the change of command ceremony and assumption of command orders. Based on the company sought, the translated title may relate better to a managing director knowing that flag officers are commonly associated as CEOs for the corporate level of the Army. For an enlisted person, a first sergeant could be an executive officer, deputy director, etc., depending on the unit's structure.

For O6 and below staff organizations, you could consider yourself a managing director, director, deputy director, senior manager, etc., depending on the unit's structure. At flag officer level organization, titles such as vice president, assistant vice president, etc., are appropriate. CEO is common for a commanding general and chief operations officer or chief administration officer based on strategic oversight. A chief of staff may possess the label president given the day-to-day operational oversight.

For a command sergeant major, command chief warrant officer, and deputy chief of staff, the title executive vice president is customary due to their executive oversight. As for aide-de-camp, secretary of the general staff, and executive officer, the title assistant vice president aligns with the direct executive support services provided. However, when in doubt, only pick or create a title relating to the industry-specific roles, responsibilities, and organizational size you seek.

Although you may have a title similar to someone of lesser or greater rank and years of service than you, what articulates the difference is the unit descriptor and your quantified bullets. For example, a small business owner and larger business owner are both CEOs, but the business descriptions (e.g., operating budget, assets, operations, etc.) are vastly different, making it necessary to include individual roles and responsibilities. Never shortchange yourself to satisfy the translation expectation the military-affiliated 14% may possess—worry about the other 80% offering jobs.

Note: Always modify your titles based on the population you're engaging (e.g., military, military affiliated, non-military). To overcome presumptions by military-affiliated persons, be sure to clearly articulate how leading, managing, and/or supporting in a conventional, special, or joint assignment varies. For example, managing a headquarters company for an O5, O6, or flag officer requires different skill levels. Moreover, depending on the organization type, the position rank may differ based on the skills required. Additionally, the span of control, composition of workforce, accountable assets, etc., may drastically vary as well even though the rank and position title are the same.

Descriptor.

The second bullet underneath the unit descriptor should be your title definer.

Assets. You should always list assets in two (2) ways. First, hard and soft. Second, direct and indirect. Soft assets represent the intangible property (e.g., people, skills, knowledge) you led, developed, managed, and supported. A basic method of associating a monetary value is via the military's Service members' Group Life Insurance and Family Service members' Group Life Insurance (e.g., $400K for service members, $100K for spouses, $10K for children) and any known value of training and leadership development pipelines (e.g., $10K for a school, $10M for a special skill). For example, an aviation command with 100 members compared to that of a personnel services command will possess drastically different soft asset values due to the training pipeline and sustainment training required. Those in command positions are also responsible for the family members of service members, so don't forget to factor that into your soft asset value.

Hard assets refer to anything tangible that you are responsible for, such as accountable items (e.g., inventory, equipment, etc.) and anything else given to you to perform your duties (e.g., a work phone, computer, desk, chair, vehicle, etc.). For example, the computer software or camera you bought or signed for is considered a hard asset because it enables you to perform your duties. As for direct and indirect assets, the actual people reporting to you and tangible items used to perform your duties are your direct assets. Thus, indirect assets refer to the soft and hard assets of organizations and communities your role and responsibilities supported. For example, a staff member is usually supporting either the unit or its subordinate elements. Whereas the command team is generally supporting an external population.

Reports. Always highlight the direct and indirect reports you are responsible for, as well as their significance. Although you worked as a team, you were expected to provide verbal and written information to key stakeholders (e.g., superiors, peers, subordinates) in various different formats. Thus, a direct report refers to any information you had to generate or forward over on a recurring basis. An indirect report refers to any information you required on a recurring basis from stakeholders that did not constitute your direct report.

Action Bullets.

These demonstrate value. Always start a bullet with what you did (e.g., directed, informed, persuaded, allocated, assessed, etc.). For some people, identifying what they did within a team is difficult. In that case, think of what someone else would have had to do if you were not present. Articulate why your actions were required (e.g., to mitigate, enhance, improve, increase, remove, etc.) and the performance impact it created (e.g., improved processes 10%); otherwise you may signal a waste of resources. To further enhance the significance of your actions, you can add monetary quantification.

Businesses ultimately care about the bottom line and how much money you saved or made, whether in actual dollars or labor-hours. For example, $20 an hour with 400 labor-hours annually saved equates to $8,000 saved. When in doubt of the monetary value for an action, list the number of labor-hours saved (preferably on an annual basis). Keep in mind, companies want to know your role and how your operating methods will transfer into their areas of need in hopes of duplicating similar success. Thus, it is imperative that every bullet provided specifies the benefit of your actions in either money surplus or labor-hours saved.

Now that your experience is fleshed out on paper, identify your value proposition (e.g., renown skills, traits, etc.). Generate a maximum of eight (8) descriptors that are not similar in interpretation. For awards, provide an overview of how many you received and for what general reason.

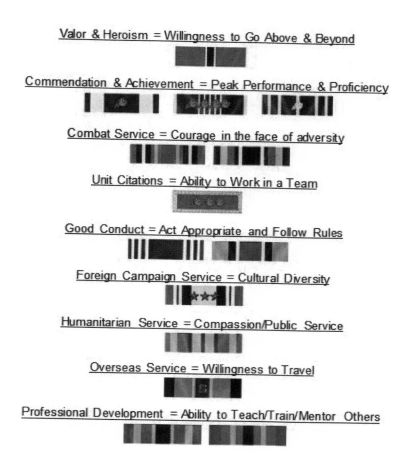

Valor & Heroism = Willingness to Go Above & Beyond

Commendation & Achievement = Peak Performance & Proficiency

Combat Service = Courage in the face of adversity

Unit Citations = Ability to Work in a Team

Good Conduct = Act Appropriate and Follow Rules

Foreign Campaign Service = Cultural Diversity

Humanitarian Service = Compassion/Public Service

Overseas Service = Willingness to Travel

Professional Development = Ability to Teach/Train/Mentor Others

Note: Talk with leadership about tailoring your final evaluation to assist with your job search. Also, ensure you obtain a verification memo for your security clearance and retain a copy of your submission paperwork to assist with any previous address information requested on a job application.

Corporate Resume.

To create more space on the page for writing out your extensive background, adjusting the margins, font size, and spacing between lines is recommended. Once you translate your experience and credentials onto an industry-tailored two-page resume (maximum) to impress a hiring manager, be sure to go back and tweak the formatting and keywords established by the company's recruitment department. Every time you modify your resume, keep in mind filtration software is used by every job-hunting platform (e.g., Indeed, LinkedIn Jobs, ZipRecruiter, Ladders, etc.) to keyword match resumes with job descriptions and any additional data the recruiting and hiring manager desires. Thus, it is important to insert the appropriate job description buzzwords before going to the recruiter for prerequisite review.

To optimize space on the resume, find synonyms that express your thoughts in as few words as possible but utilize a dictionary to confirm the meaning. A *corporate* resume should only include the past ten (10) years of experience listed out with additional years of experience summarized in an abbreviated manner. Be sure to save space on your resume to highlight any volunteer and/or extracurricular work and accomplishments supporting your job endeavors.

Forgo listing references or the phrase "will supply upon request" as that takes up precious room on the page where more experience could be listed. Plus, it is understood that you will provide references if called upon to supply them. However, create a separate document for five (5) references you have approval to use. Also, ensure you inform these five references of any jobs you supplied their name to as a reference so they are prepared to speak on your behalf if contacted to do so.

When listing the one- or two-word skills and attributes summarizing your overall innate abilities, ensure they are verifiably bound to happen regardless of the climate and culture (e.g., your rank, role, unit, etc.). As for your summary or objective, write it upon completing your resume so it serves as an executive summary or abstract of the duty titles, action bullets, and credentials therein.

LARIMEN 'LARRY' WALLACE II

Mailing Address
Phone Number
Email Address
https://www.linkedin.com/in/larrywallacejr

PROFESSIONAL SUMMARY

Seeking opportunities to serve near Austin, Texas, within Education, Healthcare, Philanthropy, or Politics. I possess 18+ years of corporate stewardship interacting and collaborating with multiple levels of management and diverse cultural audiences within complex high-tempo environments. I consistently increased workforce productivity by 20% through long-term action-oriented plans that effectively streamlined process, enhanced efficiency, and strengthened brand recognition.

SKILLS / ATTRIBUTES

- Change Management
- Human Capital Development
- Project / Lean Management
- Diversity / Inclusion
- Strategizing / Best Business Practices
- HR / Operational Metrics

CERTIFICATIONS / MEMBERSHIPS

- Lean Six Sigma - Green Belt
- Project Management Training (Syracuse University)
- Small Business Operations (Texas A&M University)
- Business Plan & Venture Pitching (St. Joseph University)
- Business Skills Foundations (University of Pennsylvania)
- Innovation & Leadership (University of Texas at Austin)
- American College of Healthcare Executives
- National Association of Healthcare Services Executives
- Golden Key International Honour Society
- Delta Mu Delta International Honor Society in Business

EDUCATION

Doctor of Philosophy: Business Administration, Northcentral University
Master of Business Administration: Management, Northcentral University ← No date of GPA
Master of Science: Human Relations and Business, Amberton University
Bachelor of Arts: Organizational Leadership, University of Texas at Arlington
Associate of Arts: General Studies, Central Texas College

PROFESSIONAL EXPERIENCE

Director of Veterans Affairs & Leadership Programs (2018 - Present)
University of Texas System - Fortune 100 Equivalent
                                                                    Austin, Texas

- Ranked #1 in Texas & Nation's 2nd largest system with 8 academic & 6 health science campuses, 216K students, 100K employees, and $24B endowment issuing 1/3rd (undergraduate) & 2/3rd (healthcare) of Texas' degrees. Top 10 most innovative system.
- Collaborated with Organizational Effectiveness, Academic & Health Affairs, Research, Faculty & Student Advisory Councils enhancing the climate & culture of veteran support 50% by realigning and identifying program needs & resources required.
- Served as veteran lead to government agencies, veteran service organization, nonprofit and corporate entities at the City, State, and National levels increasing collaboration & productivity by 50%
- Led the 10th Annual "All-State" Texas Veterans Higher Education Symposium, and UT Veterans Symposium enhancing services & support via increased collaboration by 50%

Deputy Chief of Staff **(2015 – 2017)** ← Deputy Chief of Staff Military
U.S. Army Special Operations Aviation Command (Airborne) – Fortune 100 Equivalent

Fort Bragg, North Carolina

- Increased operational capacities & strategic planning by 50% for a 4K employee (soft assets $2B+), $6.1B capital, and $750M budgeted 1-star enterprise comprising 22 departments dispersed across multiple locations servicing the Nation's most elite forces
- Regained 10K+ labor hours annually by streamlining processes as the Chief of Administration, Strategic Communications, Protocol; including Executive Officer Representative to the U.S. Army Special Operations Command (3-star Fortune 100 equivalent)
- Managed 30+ Industry, DoD & Partner Nation engagements; revised regulations, implemented human capital programs, and collaborated support efforts with the U.S. Special Operations Command (4-star) & U.S. Joint Special Operations Command (3-star)

Chief of Staff to the Chief People Officer **(2013 – 2015)** ← HR Plans and Ops Chief
U.S. Army Special Operations Aviation Command (Airborne) – Fortune 100 Equivalent

Fort Bragg, North Carolina

- Led a team of 10 (soft assets $4.5M+), directly supporting 144 employees & 4K indirectly that doubled HR strategic planning & operations for an 'all things aviation' resourcing enterprise for the U.S. Army Special Operations Command
- As the initial test unit, developed a tracking system capturing recruitment, training, assignment selection, and acclimation processes for Congress' female combat exclusion repeal initiative
- Managed critical & essential recruitment, requisition, and evaluation reports between the U.S. Army Recruiting Command (2-star, Fortune 100), U.S. Army Special Operations Command, U.S. Joint Special Operations Command, and Department of the Army
- Orchestrated a Secretary of the Army approved statue, 5+ Army Chief of Staff approved memorials, and 10+ Department of the Army annual recognitions worth $300K+ in soft assets; and improved employee satisfaction 30% via incentive & retention revisions

Larimen "Larry" Wallace II, Page 2

Managing Director **(2010 – 2013)** ← Company Commander
Bravo Company, Allied Forces North Battalion (NATO) – Fortune 100 Equivalent   Heidelberg, Germany

- Led a $400K+ capital, 120 employee company (soft assets $66.6M+) spanning 2 countries at 6 locations managing U.S. manpower to NATO Allied Forces Air & Land Commands (4 & 3-star Fortune 100's) & Center of Excellences (Czech, Ingolstadt, France, Slovakia)
- Orchestrated with U.S. European Command (4-star); Eurocorp, U.S. Army Europe & U.S. Embassies (3-stars), and Joint Center of Excellences the 1st U.S. person with family to the Czech Republic, and the future placement 7 at France & 3 at Slovakia
- Led footprint maneuvering collaborations to mitigate support gaps for a NATO Allied Forces Air Command expansion, Land Command & multiple Garrison closures, while undergoing transfer of resources and company closure concurrently
- Increased relations with 20+ partner nation 50% & regained 40K+ labor hours annually via revised resourcing processes, operating transparently, rebranding, and establishing an effective mission, task list, and human capital development process

Chief of Staff to the Chief of Intelligence / Operations Officer **(2010)** ← Deputy G2/G3
U.S. Army, NATO – Fortune 100 Equivalent   **Schweinfurt, Germany**

- Led a team of 5 (soft assets $2M+) within a 2-star enterprise overseeing antiterrorism & force protection measures for 3K+ employees with families in 12 countries at 34 locations
- Coordinated a senior executive leader's summit for 20+ U.S. general officers (1 to 3-star), senior executive service members (equivalent), Ambassadors (equivalent), and executive leaders to address & resolve quality of life issues and challenges
- Regained 200K in misused resources & enhanced the role, mission, and organizational structure via a strategic planning conference

U.S. Army / U.S. Army Reserves **(1999 – 2010)** – Fortune 500 / 1000 Equivalent   Hawaii, Texas, Germany
Platoon Leader (Managing Director - Iraq) / Drill Sergeant Training Commander (Managing Director) / Drill Sergeant (Instructor) / U.S. Army – Hawaii Customer Services Noncommissioned Officer in Charge (Senior Manager) / U.S. Army – Hawaii Centralized Promotions Board N.C.O.I.C. (Senior Manager) / U.S. Army – Hawaii Evaluations & Records Specialist / Battalion Personnel Officer (Director of People - Iraq)

ADDITIONAL EXPERIENCE

Nonprofit, Educational, and Recognitions   **Europe, Maryland, North Carolina, Texas**

- City Councilman; Employment & Training Advisory Member for Texas Veterans Commission; Higher Education Chair for Texas Military Spouse Economic Empowerment Zone (San Antonio); Chair for University of Texas' Veterans Leadership Task Force; Veterans Advisor for Travis County Commissioner Court – Precinct 1; Co-Author of The Transition: Preparing for Financial Combat
- Former Nonprofit Special Advisor to CEO of Grateful Heart – Comprehensive Veteran Services (counseling & referrals) & Former Executive in Residence for VETTED and its pilot program of 25 Veterans in partnership with UT-Austin & UPENN Wharton
- Nonprofit Vice Chairman for C2 Change (mental illness support) & Former Radio Personality for Blackberry Gospel Radio; revised 5-district and 2-national protocol manuals; developed 2 state educational programs
- President for 3 districts and 13 local bodies, a state Junior Vice President, Strategic Director for 4 states, Chief Administrative Officer for 3 national staffs, and bestowed 3 honorary and 25 invitational memberships
- International Scholar Laureate Program (Business & Entrepreneurship) recipient; Community Health Champion (Ambassador) for Travis County Healthcare Division (Central Health); 2018 Dissertation of the Year Nominee
- Adjunct Professor and Proctor for the University at Maryland University College and Central Texas College
- 2019 Austin 40 Under 40 Finalist, 27 performance / proficiency, 5 foreign relations, 3 teamwork, 3 cultural diversity, 2 adversity / courage, 2 personifications, 2 district staff members of the year, 1 community service, and 1 president of the year award
- Member of Society of Human Resource Management, Dallas Human Resource Management Association, Entrepreneurship) recipient, Association of the United States Army member, and National Defense University Joint Special Operations Masters of Art's in Strategic Studies Selectee

One-Page Resume (Wall Street).

Although a single-page resume used to be the corporate norm, it is more frequently associated with financial corporations and similar institutions. The format for this style of resume is similar to the *corporate* resume (e.g., quantifiable experience, education, training, recognitions, etc.) within the past 10 years. To condense your *corporate* resume into a *Wall Street* resume, bear down to the most important data for the opportunity. Then reword as necessary to make actions bullets even more concise and precise.

Note: Upon completing your *Wall Street resume*, review your *corporate resume* to revise for more space and additional action bullets.

Government Resume.

Unlike the one-page and two-page resumes, a *government* resume is formatted to meet the latest Office of Personnel Management (OPM) requirements, which change often. Additionally, *government* resumes are typically three (3) to seven (7) pages long due to the level of detail and information involved, which is not necessarily requested for civilian sector jobs. For example, they may request details regarding certifications and professional publications (e.g., hard copy, internet, etc.). Therefore, it is recommended that you review fedshirevets.gov and possibly hire a professional writer to ensure you meet OPM standards and incorporate all of the necessary and relevant information for desired positions.

Note: Retired pay can be withheld or forfeited if you enter into a conflict of interest per the Finance Management Policy, Military Pay Policy for Retired Pay. Any amounts withheld for accepting a foreign job without congressional consent, as required by the United States Constitution, will be treated as no entitlement and will not be "held in trust" for possible receipt in the future. When working for the civil service, you may waive your retired pay to establish eligibility and/or computation for retirement annuity.

Bio-Resume.

A bio-resume tells the rest of your story. Formatted like a biography, it highlights unique experiences a resume does not have the space to permit. This is your human factor edge when applying for a job. Oftentimes, networking events are too informal for a resume; whereas, a single-page *bio-resume* sends the appropriate message regarding your experience, credentials, and capability in a refreshing biographical story. This personal resume format will prove valuable when engaging with senior-level executives interested in you but not ready for the formalities of an interview.

Similar to the aforementioned resumes, the *bio-resume* speaks about your work experience, education, volunteer service, and extracurricular activities. However, unlike the other resumes, the *bio-resume* affords you the opportunity to highlight interesting facts about your experiences, volunteer service, and other activities. Always bring it to face-to face meetings and interviews, and send a copy electronically with your resume when permitted.

Note: Always write the *bio-resume* in as a third-person introductory narrative, include a headshot, and recognize your immediate family (e.g., married to, has a son/daughter named). If you're serious about branding yourself, the *bio-resume* is a must.

Colonel Heath Niemi is a 1992 West Point Graduate and veteran of 20 combat tours in Afghanistan and Iraq with the 160th Special Operations Aviation Regiment. Colonel Niemi is transitioning out of the military and the U.S. Army Special Operations Aviation Command (USASOAC) after 25 years of service in the spring of 2017.

Heath is currently the Chief of Staff for the commanding general of the USASOAC and in charge of a staff of 144 personnel and 22 sub-divisions (the CFO, COO, CIO, HR, acquisition, legal and medical directors report to him) that resources and trains special operation aviation to support the most elite special operations ground forces around the globe. As the portfolio director for the enterprise, Heath oversees the $750 million annual budget and the $3.9 billion Future Years Defense Program (FYDEP) for an organization composed of 4200 personnel and 204 aircraft which include specially modified helicopters, fixed wing, and unmanned systems worth in excess of $6.1 billion.

An inspirational leader, Heath is a driver of organizational change. He created the organization's knowledge management system for daily operations and programs that led to savings in time, money, and increased cross functional awareness. Additionally, he led a human resource transformation of the organization to fix manpower authorizations and streamline responsibility. On a side note, he initiated an analysis of the flying hour algorithm which led to a $130-million-dollar savings in the FYDEP.

Other unique capabilities Heath possesses is the ability to virtually lead a globally dispersed organization as he led a team (Battalion) that was employed across Iraq, Afghanistan, Asia and the U.S. simultaneously. He was also involved in the initial deployments to both Afghanistan in 2001 and Iraq in 2003, where he participated in the evolution of systems and processes to include global command and control and logistics. In combat, he was the Commander of all Joint Task Force Special Operation Army Aviation assets in theater on twelve separate deployments.

With 25 years of leadership and management experience, Heath has a masters of leadership and management as well as a masters of strategic studies from the U.S. Army War College where he studied macro geopolitical government and military strategy and was recognized as a distinguished graduate.

Other interesting notes. Heath was the only World Helicopter Team Gold Medalist for the U.S. team in 1996 and once a nationally ranked power lifter in the U.S.P.F. He created and writes a daily investment blog called Strategic Stimulus that correlates macroeconomics for day trading. He is also currently writing academic works on future methods of warfare to include autonomous drones and is working with U.S. Army War College on the future of technologically enabled leadership.

He is married to the former Michele Holmes of Nashville, Tennessee and is the proud father of two daughters, Kimber 4 and Kendall 3.

Business-Networking Card.

You should always have a *business-networking card* in addition to your *bio-resume*. Do not let an opportunity to market yourself pass you by. You are always job hunting, even when it's not an official interview. Sometimes an opportunity to network or interview sparks from a brief conversation in passing or any other unplanned engagement. For those times, it's either too unprofessional to provide a resume or you just don't have a resume on you due to their bulkiness; the ideal substitute is a *business-networking card.*

Unlike a traditional business card, the *business-networking card* informs the holder of your experience and abilities while providing your contact information and links to your social media (e.g., LinkedIn). On the card you want to include a photo to refresh the recipient's memory of who the card came from, and subsequently the engagement that occurred. Think of times you received a card from someone and when you looked at it later, you just couldn't recall the person or any details about how you received the card so you moved on and threw away the card. Don't let that be you, especially during the job-hunting phase.

Note: Insert your LinkedIn QR code on your card as an easy way for those who are tech savvy to quickly look you up and learn more about you.

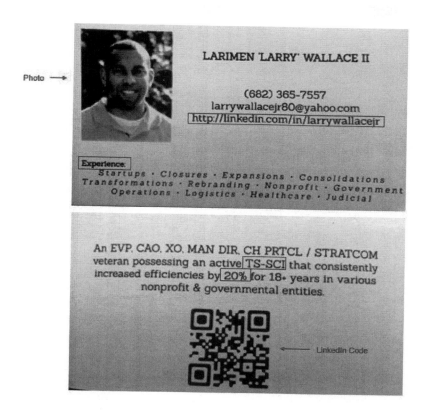

LinkedIn Profile (LI).

Getting your *LI* profile completed needs to happen right after finishing your resume; this is one of the very first items on your job search roadmap. Of all the social platforms for job-hunting, *LI* is probably the most powerful online tool. Where else can you look for and apply to jobs, establish a robust professional profile, target search for people connected to your areas of interest, and then reach out to them directly? *LI* is so highly utilized that most job postings permit you to use your *LI* profile in lieu of inserting your personal data and/or resume. Therefore, your *LI* profile should serve as your electronic resume that enables you to expound upon any volunteer services, extracurricular activities, recognitions, etc., not appropriate for a physical resume.

Having an *LI* account is critical to your success because most professionals, especially hiring managers, pre-screen and vet candidates via *LI* and any other social media platforms to learn more about you. You can bet that LinkedIn is the first-place employers and human resource divisions go to look you up. The reverse is true as well. Job seekers find using LinkedIn to get to know a possible employer, company, and interviewers to be invaluable. Ensure you use it for every job search engagement.

Before you upgrade to a premium account, sign up for your free Veteran premium upgrade, which lasts for 12 months and is reusable. The benefit of a premium account is the ability to monitor who viewed your profile. To enhance utilization of your *LI* account, go to https://www.linkedin.com/pulse/how-veterans-can-make-most-out-linkedin-daniel-savage.

Note: Only list GPAs that are 3.7 or higher and extracurricular activities with the credential you pursued, and consolidate awards and certificates of appreciation/commendation to mitigate a cumbersome profile.

Email Account.

Ensure your email address is respectable and reflects professionalism. Never send an email without a signature block, whether you are composing it or replying to one received. A traditional signature block will begin a line stating "Thank you," "Respectfully," or

"V/R" for "Very respectfully." Subsequently, on a few lines below will be your preferred work name, phone number, email address, and LinkedIn account information.

Note: Ensure the email server you use (e.g., Gmail, Yahoo!, iCloud, etc.) is not something outdated, which may inadvertently expose the fact that you are not experienced with current technology.

TRANSITION PSYCHOLOGY

Pre-Contract—The Transition.

Regardless of when you start your transition, be prepared for one thing...to put in work. Be mentally prepared for the stress and strain of *working and transitioning in your spare time.* Even the DoD lengthened the transition window to 24 months to help mitigate burnout. Do not let the culmination point of your service be the most stressful and least productive due to overexerting at both ends of the stick.

Expectation management is key. Networking not only takes time, but patience. It must happen naturally. You will find opportunities to connect during your usual vocations and outings. Early stage connections will most likely be introductions and mentorship in preparation for your 90–120 availability window. Never allow yourself to get frustrated when people fail to call or reply in a timely manner. Always assume they are extremely busy and view the time they take to connect, mentor, and/or consider you as an opportunity—something to be grateful for, rather than something to expect. Be grateful for others' time, and expect things to take time.

Before you begin any follow-ups, create a network diagram of who connected you to whom to effectively update them or remind them of their efforts for you and how you have maximized their efforts for your regard. Following up is especially important for early stage connections that were initially outside the 90–120 day hiring window.

Being unconfined to a specific geographical location or industry is a blessing for the vast array of opportunities available to you and a curse because you must filter those opportunities to what is in your best interest. Know that finding where your optimal satisfaction may reside may cause stress when you possess a nonspecific technical skill (e.g., aviation, medical, health, lawyer, etc.). Therefore, you must consider where your domain knowledge and experience reside. Some initial areas of opportunity are the defense sector due to your military comprehension and security clearance. Or some general form of leadership, management (e.g., operations, program, project) with anyone willing to accept you. Keep in mind, the further you venture from your domain knowledge and experiences, the less transferrable skills you possess to enhance your value proposition.

Always keep an open discussion with your loved ones especially on anything significant, because they are part of your decision cycle. By keeping your loved ones situationally aware, some stress common with establishing household financial security can be reduced. A way to keep everyone up-to-date and on time for making a critical decision is a roadmap and a calendar. Although 18 months seems like a long time to plan, it will pass by quickly. You could feel unprepared to separate even with 60 or more days of accrued leave if you don't track the time carefully.

Note: We highly recommend creating an 18-month roadmap timeline in order to keep track of important requirements and events.

Transition Roadmap

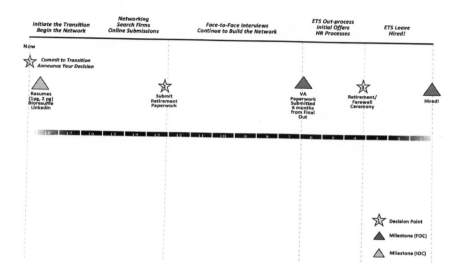

Post Contract—Opportunity Found.

Based on your situation (i.e., duty assignment, position, etc.), your transition psychology experience will possess minor differences, although overall it will be similar to many others who have transitioned before you and will make the transition after you.

Know the first four (4) months of transition is exciting due to the new challenges, experiences, and knowledge accrued. However, the comradery, response times, and formalities are vastly different in Corporate America. Thus, having hobbies and extracurricular activities are critical to support the management of your heightened expectations. For example, phone calls and emails outside of work hours (e.g., traditionally 8:00 am to 5:00 pm, Monday through Friday) are frowned upon, and most people will respond only when they have an answer to your inquiry.

The next four (4) months is commonly when you begin to use your military experiences to push through on self-interests, professional obligations, etc., although you may dislike your situation. At this stage, the onset of self-doubting your choices and uncertainty in how to proceed (e.g., revising your approach, staying or leaving, etc.) begin. Oftentimes you will stay to push through under an obligatory mentality instilled by the military. However, as a civilian, you must take care of you unless under a binding contract. Unlike the military, you can be fired on short notice if in the best interest of the company. Thus, as a civilian you should always make decisions in the best interest of yourself and loved ones.

The final four (4) months become personally critical because unmanaged stress could cause illness or outward displays of dissatisfaction. Moreover, untreated depression may not only hinder your work or job-hunting efforts and family cohesion, but it can cause unexpected health and mental issues. Understand that you and your family are now the most important factors in your life and that this new civilian marketplace may not become the close-knit community you once were a part of. Look for the positive facets of your new job and take the opportunity to learn and grow from all that is available.

Whenever you encounter a negative situation, such as a difficult boss, reflect on your various leaders in the military and how you diplomatically worked with them. If you decide to change jobs, do not feel guilty—most new veterans test the waters at several locations until they learn what they are truly comfortable with.

Once you land your first job, stay at least 12 to 18 months for work history purposes. Additionally, mitigate large employment gaps via volunteer work, maybe interning to gain industry experience, or developing a weak skill or desired skill via training, education, and lower-level positions. Maybe even start a limited liability company (LLC) to dabble with consulting in your area of expertise between full-time occupations. You may find that your LLC could become your full-time option.

Note: Do not incorporate your transition leave into your 18 to 24-month transition process. When possible, never hinder your employment window and opportunities. Unless you desire to work for the Department of Defense, you don't have to wait until you exit the military to start working.

THE FACTORS

The following list of factors are things to consider when framing your job opportunities. Identify what matters to you the most and why. If you could move anywhere in the world, where would you most want to be? If you want to continue in your technical skillset, in what capacity? Which is more important—location or compensation? Being with family or climbing the corporate ladder? A small or large company? Being a business owner or having a boss to guide you? By taking these factors into consideration, you will find a multitude of options and paths that are appealing.

There are eleven (11) factors to consider and prioritize before searching for opportunities, when opportunities present themselves to you, and when opportunities are offered. Although the following factors are **NOT** in any particular order, you should establish your preferred order of merit list (OML): Role, Flexibility, Geography, Compensation, Quality of Life, Autonomy, Engagement, Quality of the Team, Risk, Company Size, and Diversity. As you create your OML, discuss it with your loved ones so there is an agreement on what is best for the family. Be sure to revisit your OML at least monthly to revise it as needed, based on changing circumstances.

Apply your order of merit list (OML) to any job opportunities, to help you frame the factors to consider. Most service members can go anywhere within the United States or abroad and perform a myriad of jobs, if given the opportunity. The leadership and management (human capital development), project and program expertise, along with your profession's demand of arms soft and hard skills (tangible and intangible) literally make you an asset in any industry—if placed appropriately. Therefore, it can be overwhelming to identify your post-military passion; but it is a good idea to have one!

How do you establish parameters to focus only on things of importance to you and your family? For example, maybe compensation truly outweighs location because of aging parents; maybe the people you work with outranks company status; or maybe being your own boss outranks a loss of autonomy from having a boss. By incorporating the following factors into your OML (decision making process), opportunities truly worthy of your time are quickly identified without bias, undue influence, or immediate needs. You may even find the ideal job is down an unbeaten path that your credentials and experience are perfect for.

Although the following prioritization list will differ per person, the 30 minutes allocated to identify, justify, and approve your wants and desires with loved ones via the OML mitigates tremendous stress. As stated previously, ensure you revisit the OML every four (4) weeks or so, as new circumstances may change rankings.

Role.

To ensure you apply for and accept positions complementary to your years of professional military education and on-the-job training, you must analyze your military assignments to appropriately select the relevant, relative civilian terms of the desired industry. For example, a vice president in business has a very different level of influence in banking, while titles in tech companies like Dell can be misleading on the level of technical expertise required. Thus, once you identify the appropriate civilian titles appropriate to your military assignments, the next crucial step is identifying one to three things you consistently did at each assignment that enabled you to be successful—your *individual strengths*.

Your *individual strengths* are how—no matter the situation and circumstances—you are consistently known for operating in a certain manner to succeed. Your *individual strengths* are no different than that of Coca-Cola or any other business striving to have something that is similar to, but better than, their competitors; meaning, the proprietary manner in which you think, act, and execute in jobs of similar roles and responsibilities as your peers is unique to you. Therefore, where do you constantly succeed (leading, managing, staff work, etc.)? Moreover, identify the ratio between your two lines of success (i.e., 75% leading, 25% staff) and level of autonomy (i.e., 75% empowerment, 25% micro-management).

Once you determine suitable jobs by desired industry, your next effort is comprehending which roles meet informal prerequisites, provide desired opportunities, and accelerate careers; in addition to assessing the type of compensation, pay, and benefits needed or desired. Keep in mind, greater responsibility means greater liability, so it is recommended to stay within your areas of domain knowledge (e.g., significant areas of expertise) to mitigate loss in confidence by stakeholders.

Usage of titles can accelerate your civilian opportunities and success; notably, the opposite is true if you overreach and underperform. For example, a vice president in the banking industry is parallel to a manager within the defense industry; however, a vice president in defense would be comparable to a managing director in banking. Therefore, know the titles and the level of responsibility associated with them before you apply for a job—the understanding of such words is imperative.

Always strive to attain roles and responsibilities that are at least equivalent to your rank. The ramifications of taking a lower level of responsibilities is that it may take you three (3) to five (5) years to arrive to the acknowledgement of the skill set you held from the outset of leaving the military. Just know that obtaining a job equal to your military capability is not easy and sometimes requires more time and effort than expected. Because jobs don't wait around for you, you must search them out and cast your net wide.

Flexibility.

Because your first, second, or even third job outside the military may not be "just the right fit," accept a position with evident opportunity for progression. Flexibility within a company is something you must assess based upon the number of years you plan to work before civilian retirement. Is moving up, or even laterally, feasible? If so, what is the general timeline? Regardless of the company's size, always review the organizational structure (overall and departmental) to be well informed on where you would reside and probable flexibility afforded. Also, look at the various different sectors you could move into at a later time.

Smaller companies will have less opportunities to do this, and mid-size companies may be a nice fit; however, generally large primes will have more opportunity for you to move or grow into your future profession. Thus, smaller companies may possess less flexibility in decision making, expenses incurred, work-life balance, etc., because of the bottom-line needed to sustain operations and existence until growth. Larger companies generally have more health and growth (economic maturity).

Don't forget about startups as they may enable you to quickly become an organizational decision maker, although the layers of leadership are flat given the few employees it holds until it grows. You may find that if you can get in on the ground floor of a startup you may have the ability to rise quite rapidly into the decision maker that you strive to be, but on the flip side there is usually a tighter pyramid to climb initially until the company starts to grow. There is also an element of risk that you may want to consider.

Geography.

A person's or family's time horizon for a final retirement location, aging parents, and children in high school are all factors that may focus or limit a transitioning soldier. If confined or limited to a certain location, it can limit opportunities. On the upside, these limitations can focus the job search. For those without geographic constraints and with a willingness to move, other considerations need to be taken into account. For example, geography plays a crucial role in the post-military salary needed to maintain your current military lifestyle. If you are a resident of a state without income tax, depending on where you move upon separation your retired pay, interest, etc., will be taxed in addition to your federal tax. A great place to compare costs of living is bankrate.com.

For example, in 2017, the cost of living in Fayetteville, NC, at $104,000 averaged the same amount for Austin, TX, with variations in amenity (e.g., housing, food, etc.) expenses; whereas a $104,000 salary in Fayetteville required a 38% increase ($143,553) to maintain the same lifestyle in Washington, DC. Therefore, it is recommended to always perform a cost of living comparison for intended living locations, interviews scheduled, and job offers received. It is a wake-up call to find oneself in a state like North Carolina, that has a large retired military population, to realize that North Carolina taxes your income at 5.45% as well as your military pension at 5.45%. A great place to compare costs of living is bankrate.com.

Income & Military Pension Nontax. Alaska, Florida, Nevada, New Hampshire, South Dakota, Tennessee, Texas, Washington, Wyoming.

Taxed Retired Pay. Alabama, Connecticut, Hawaii, Illinois, Kansas, Louisiana, Massachusetts, Michigan, Mississippi, New Jersey, New York, Ohio, Pennsylvania, Wisconsin.

Other Taxes. New Hampshire and Tennessee both tax interest and dividends at a 5% flat rate.

Compensation.

Obviously, compensation is a very important factor to contemplate when transitioning out of the military. Do you have military retirement to help cushion the day after your final out? Will you have disability compensation? What lifestyle do you want to maintain and achieve? What personal expenses are you going to have, such as a child's education/college tuition? Are you expected to support an ailing parent? Are you jump-starting a new business? These are all types of subcomponents that may need to be considered when assessing how important compensation may be to your path forward. Later on, the book will discuss negotiating your *total compensation* based on pay and benefits sought.

Too often, service members assess their post-military financial needs for a sustained standard of living incorrectly. After obtaining your military compensation and pay statement from your MyPay account, you will see exactly what other well-being services and benefits the military is covering and what may be out-of-pocket expenses for you. For example, your leave and earnings statement may add up to $80,000 in salary annually, but your compensation and pay statement when including commissary, exchange, health, and dental benefits equate to $104,000.

Before you start thinking about the *total compensation* you deserve, first identify what you will receive via pension, VA disability rating, and any other permanent money streams for a base standard of living budget (e.g., secure from periods of unemployment). After subtracting your post-military monetary benefits from your overall salary per the compensation and pay statement, the difference is what you must make to sustain your current lifestyle. For example, a disability rating of 80% with spouse and child is $1,816.25 plus retired pay at $2,000 a month (i.e., $1,816.25 + $2,000 = $3,816.25 * 12 = $45,795) minus your current military earnings and compensation of $104,000, means a post-military salary of $58,205 is needed. Thus, any pay above $58,205 means you're paid more than if you stayed in the military; however, this is your worst-case scenario.

Regardless of how well you know your financials, go see a professional financial advisor and estate planner. Take the time to give the advisor as much of your financial data as possible in order to lay out where you currently stand compared to your future financial expectations. If you expect to live on a gross income of $150,000 in today's dollars, think of inflation and the devaluation of your money over time. Use the financial advisor to account for your retired pay, disability compensation, your assets, etc., to give you a snapshot of where you are today and how much is needed to meet your goals now and in the future. You may already be there, *or you may realize you need a whole lot more than expected.* Regardless, you are now pointed in the right direction for pursuit of the right opportunity.

The best-case scenario is obtaining a salary equal to or more than your total military pay; thereby enabling your military pension, disability pay, and any other permanent money received from military service to be available as cash. Although your military experiences may not enable you to obtain a pay near your total military salary, the closer to it you are, the less your post-military benefits serve as compensation rather than as surplus. When assessing what your post-military salary goal should be, research your peers (e.g., rank, years of service, experience, credentials, location, etc.) based on industries of interest and job type.

You may not fall into this category, but it seems the topic of pay is kryptonite to some service members, making it perhaps the most important topic to consider when transitioning out of the military. By assessing compensation head-on, you can avoid unpleasant surprises in later years.

Quality of Life.

The definition of quality depends on the individual. Thus, being self-aware of what lifestyle you must have or that you desire for yourself and your loved ones is crucial to post-military career satisfaction. If you end up working a similar schedule for similar compensation and pay as your military career, you might as well have stayed in the military if you elected to separate. The basic quality of life expectation upon separating from the military should be obtaining compensation, pay, and benefits close to those received while serving, having a less stressful work schedule, and gaining a new association with a company whose culture and climate enables you to flourish.

In addition to the duty assignment quality-of-life aspects mentioned, there are environmental aspects to equally consider. Begin assessing your final move location no less than 18 months out to make informed decisions that impact your personal finances and happiness. For example, what locations are in the growth business cycle of your desired profession and industry? What daycare and school districts are desirable for preschool and school-age kids? Annual weather? Location in regards to family, close friends, and access points to easily and inexpensively travel?

Autonomy.

The degree to which you have freedom of autonomy within a company may be highly desirable. Does the job opportunity empower you to make timely decisions on behalf of the company? Are you in a role that allows you to make decisions affecting company policy and strategy? In some cases, the desire for freedom of autonomy may translate into owning your own business. Either way, this factor holds a far-reaching effect on your roadmap. Consider how significant this value is to you.

Engagement.

What do you want your daily workday to look like? How busy do you want your schedule to be? What level of challenge do you want professionally? Determine how much traveling you prefer, type of locations, and the kind of people you'd most like to interact with and how. How much work-life balance do you prefer to stay more engaged with your loved ones? Do you like business-to-business transactions, mingling with other business professionals, etc.?

Whether you realize it or not, in the military you have served in a highly stressful and fully engaged profession that required you to stay at peak performance throughout the duration. With every permanent change of station (PCS) you experienced (i.e., yourself, superiors, peers, subordinates), you had to demonstrate a level of technical proficiency and leadership to receive the evaluations and assignments you desired. Ensure that you identify the level and types of engagement you desire in a career after the military, as this factor heavily connects to stress.

Quality of the Team.

The quality of interactions you have with the people you work with—especially your boss—is critical to your mental health when you transition into your first commercial experience. There is a certain amount of stress that the unknown, or a toxic supervisor, or constant friction with stakeholders can cause. Although quality is what you perceive, identify what common values, levels of respect, displays of professionalism, and overall culture you expect. A high value in *Quality of Team* is quite often what draws veterans to work with other military-affiliated companies. However, lots of companies possess a great culture, work ethic/mission focus, and cohesiveness beyond these common choices. In any case, never judge a book by its cover. Make sure you do due diligence and research the company you are considering working for, because your mental health is equally tied to both your lifestyle and work environment.

Risk.

Risk is associated with almost every factor under consideration here, and is therefore perhaps one of the more important factors. Smaller companies and startups are simply riskier than medium-sized companies needing immediate results, and larger companies that can afford to train you. As for the roles you seek, the greater the responsibility, the greater the liability. Thus, how much risk are you willing to take overall and within each different factor? Are you risk-averse? Of course, trying to get your ideal job out of the military assumes some risk as you ponder different opportunities. Luckily, you can offset risk with great financial and transition plans.

Knowing the environment (e.g., type of people) you prefer to work with (e.g., demographics, professional standpoints, philanthropic, esprit de corps, etc.) is essential to ensuring your post-military career path starts off successfully. As in the military, a trend of short-term jobs is frowned upon and may detract from the experience you offer. Therefore, ensure jobs that are lower than your perceived worth can be easily tied to a value, such as learning a new skill, experimenting with an assumed ideal job, a strong financial need for the income, etc. Whether you decide to work for an organization with a high military makeup or even a Department of Defense related organization, times of suffering through an undesirable workplace are up to you, given the absence of a military service obligation and any pension, compensation, and/or disability the military is paying.

Company Size.

There are numerous pros and cons to consider before applying for and accepting a job position. For small companies and startups (e.g., team, company, squadron, etc.), opportunities of increasing roles of responsibility and the ability to acquire stock/equity stake (e.g., 5% ownership) resulting in greater net worth are higher. Just ensure that you are informed of the rules, policies, and vesting period for any stock/equity. However, the rate of bankruptcy and layoffs is equally high given the limited market share (e.g., 1% of the local industry) that small organizations frequently possess. Unless you see evidence-based potential for growth, be cautious.

Medium companies are more established but are often not extremely efficient. However, opportunities for a role of greater responsibility are increased. Just know there may be an expectation to perform rather rapidly. Additionally, medium companies are prone to re-organization as they grow internally, adding on sectors or cutting out entire departments. Large companies are often the best place to learn because they are big enough to overcome small training mistakes. However, getting roles of great responsibility come more through networking than the must-fill scenarios associated with small and medium companies. When dealing with company size, there is quite a bit to consider.

Do not fall for the fallacy of thinking larger organizations pay more or that getting to the top is easier in smaller organizations. Most of the time, pay and upward mobility are associated with the phase of the business cycle (e.g., growth, expansion, maturity, or exit stage) the company is in, so do your research.

Note: What constitutes a small, medium, and large company is based on the industry you seek to enter. Also, the influence of decision making within Corporate America is very similar to military bureaucracy. Influencing change at a team, company, or squadron level is significantly easier and swifter to implement than a flag/general officer command.

Diversity.

What is it that you would like to do post-military? Depending on your specialty, you could perform a similar job in almost any organization. Do you want to stay in DoD, switch to local or state government, not-for-profit, nonprofit, for-profit, etc.? What type of industry and sector within that industry appeal to you?

Based on your interests, whether hobby or otherwise, search for opportunities that align with your passions. For example, are you interested in future disruptive technologies that may offer untold opportunities (i.e., drones, virtual reality, big data, cyber, etc.)? Whatever it may be, do your research on the company's annual report for their vision, mission, profit/loss summary, and initiatives. What a company says and what is actually occurring is proven or disproven within annual reports.

NEGOTIATING TOTAL COMPENSATION

One of the hardest topics to negotiate in your interview process is the question of compensation. During your interview process, you never know when you may be asked what compensation you are looking for and what your overall compensation was in your last occupation. For the latter, if pressured to answer, pull out your overall compensation notice from your service that you used to laugh about. Now it is vitally important. For many of us, medical and dental benefits are just something we were peripherally aware of in the background, more of a pain in the rear based on the requirement to complete annual physicals and shots. However, medical and dental is now a large sum of money you can use for negotiating compensation.

You will notice on your compensation sheet that given all of these sundry pays that your overall compensation was quite a bit larger than imagined…but at the same time most likely still quite off from what your peers in the civilian sector receive for the same roles, responsibilities, and risk. Always know what you are being paid in total by the military and what those of your civilian counterparts are being paid in total, because some companies inquire about your desired pay. Never answer a pay inquiry question until you are in the final rounds of selection.

Attempt to inquire on what their usual pay for similar positions is and what the range for that particular job is. As numbers begin to be tossed around, inquire how health, dental, and other military benefits you retain will be captured in the pay because it's not a company coverage need. Another good tip when negotiating is to remember 20 days of paid time off (PTO) equals the 30 days of leave you received in the military. A way to address this time off is to relay how it is something you and your family are accustomed to.

Other pays to consider on top of your base pay are: pregnancy leave, sick days, 401K, 401K matching, bonuses (annual, sales, etc.), medical and dental insurance, equity (e.g., actual ownership, stock options, etc.), relocation bonus, signing bonus, compensated education (e.g., higher education, technical school, etc.). As for special incentives, they could include a professional advisor like Goldman Sachs to manage your portfolio, etc.

As we go through each of these other pays, remember there are countless variations:

Medical & Dental.

For many of us, medical and dental coverage were benefits provided to us while serving even if we were unaware that it was accounted for in our annual compensation and earnings statement. Aside from any Veterans Health Administration coverage you may receive as a 50% or above disabled veteran or initial first 5 years free before co-pays are required, factor 10% of your pay for proper coverages. To mitigate the potential loss of benefit due to a lack of coverage at your new job, inquire for a compensation increase equal to the cost of coverages for dependents on the company's insurance package.

Note: Always keep your Tricare Health, Tricare Dental, and Veterans Life (e.g., veterans group, service-disabled, veterans mortgage) insurances as they stay with you no matter where you go; insurance provided by an employer terminates upon your departure.

Paid Time Off (PTO).

When calculating whether the appropriate amount of annual time off is being offered by your potential employer, consider that the usual 30 days of earned leave is lowered to around 20 days post-military. Also, be cognizant that the usual three- and four-day weekends attached to holiday observances may drastically decrease. Be able to clearly articulate why you need a certain amount of interchangeable leave or sick days to maintain an accustomed work-life balance.

Note: The more monthly compensation received for retirement and/or disability, the more pertinent it is to establish your expectations early on to mitigate frustration and stress due to working in an undesirable situation.

Relocation.

Because the military will cover your last permanent change of station, request any relocation funds a company offers to be provided as a bonus, to cover short-term housing, hotels, baby/dog sitters, food, etc. You will not be compensated for this as you have in the past when the military moved you, so try to negotiate a moving bonus from your company as part of your financial package.

Before buying a house, ensure you do so months before receiving your final leave and earnings (LES) statement as financial institutions look at what you will be making not what you made to ensure you can pay the loan back. If after thorough research you are still unable to identify an ideal living location, rent to permit yourself to get a true lay of the land before buying a place you may regret.

Education & Training.

Similar to the military's tuition assistance and professional military education system, most companies will support your organization, industry, and personal professionalism pursuit. Always inquire about modes of compensating your training to mitigate out-of-pocket expenses, especially if training is specifically geared towards improving your productivity and enhancing your efficiency on the job.

401K and Matching.

Most companies offer a 401K plan, and most offer some sort of matching plan. Generally, an employer will contribute 3% to 6% of an employee's pay if the employee contributes a certain percentage into the company's 401K plan. Always take advantage of this tax-deferred retirement program.

Sign-On Bonus.

Some companies will offer you a sign-on bonus as an incentive to accept their offer of employment over other opportunities. If they don't, go ahead and counteroffer with a sign-on bonus. The bonus size will largely depend on your role in the company.

Stock/Equity Options—Vesting period.

Equity is the key to generational wealth. Whether it is in the form of stock options in a publicly traded company or actual (%) percentage partnership in a private firm, ownership is the way to speed up the capture of your and your family's financial goals.

Sales/Performance Bonus.

For those that take on a sales or business development role, the front office (the money-making division of the company) is usually incentivized with sales bonuses. Ensure that it is clearly spelled out in your contract how sales/performance bonuses are rewarded.

Other Miscellaneous Compensation.

For certain sales jobs, you can receive a free vehicle every 60,000 miles to include gas/maintenance/insurance. Sales benefits may include trips, all expenses paid. Sales point systems can convert to gifts and bonuses, such as house buyback and resale. Some companies will assist in a house purchase, spousal placement assistance, or

1-year of executive coaching. The list can go on and on and be very unique to the opportunity at hand to include first-class travel over certain distances, jet service, etc.

Note: Never be afraid to ask for a perk but do so based on research. Unlike the military, human capital and leadership development are not the driving force but rather what you were hired for. Thus, you must become more proactive in identifying funding and compensation opportunities not openly communicated.

ENTREPRENEUR / CONSULTING

Independence! Some of you may want to dive into a passion, area of expertise, or a concept developed over time. You are now free to take the time and risk to develop your business venture, whether brick and mortar, a service-based business, or internet-based endeavor. However, it is notable to mention advice by Michael Gerber from his book *Entrepreneurial Myth*, which says commonplace assumptions can get in the way of running a business. Beware that owning your own business, such as consulting, doesn't always enable complete independence.

Although you may be able to establish your own hours, control the taking on of clients, and decide income, doing so heavily depends upon you establishing and maintaining market share throughout the business cycle. Furthermore, depending upon your small business operations knowledge (e.g., marketing, branding, finance, business operations, corporate finance, etc.) and those you can bring on to elevate your efforts, you must continuously perform SWOT analyses (e.g., strengths, weaknesses, opportunities, threats) to overcome business competition via Porter's Five Forces (e.g., competitive rivalry, supplier power, buyer power, threat of substitution, threat of new entry).

Some of the primary concerns with a business startup are your mental fortitude and expectation management. This will be extremely hard work, most likely some of the hardest work you have done in your life short of a live combat engagement. The financial and personal risk alone that a startup will incur only adds another layer of hard work and stress. Overwhelming senses will likely occur due to wearing so many different hats for the business to stay afloat and thrive.

There is fallacy in thinking that owning your own business guarantees the independence to come and go as you please and make decisions on your discretion alone. The hours you work are based on your clients, which you must please to bring in the income needed. Establishing market share will require long, demanding days, often with no true payoff in sight. As your business passes through each stage of the business life cycle, you must relearn how to efficiently and effectively run your operation.

Small Business Operations.

Depending on your corporate and small business operations knowledge (e.g., marketing, branding, finance, business operations, corporate finance, etc.), your risk of business ownership failure is increased. For example, how in-depth can you operate QuickBooks, conduct a profit/loss statement, or manage a cash flow file? Do you know how to create a business canvas before executing a business plan to ensure your way forward is not only unique but operates under Lean Six Sigma and project management basics?

Note: Before executing a contract for services or a product, know your overall cost and expense for individual line items to provide that service or product. At minimum, whether for-profit, nonprofit, or not-for-profit, you must be at a break-even operating model.

Competition Assessments.

In the military, you frequently received an operations order, performed rock drills, and rehearsed before executing the true mission. Starting a business requires the same fortitude and temperament, which will result in success. For your business idea, you should conduct a SWOT analysis (e.g., strengths, weaknesses, opportunities, threats) before spending one cent on the business except for data collection. If you determine the idea is viable, test your business concept via Porter's Five Forces (e.g., competitive rivalry, supplier power, buyer power, threat of substitution, threat of new entry).

Note: A business idea and business concept are separate functions leading to the generation of a business plan. Whether you plan to provide a product (e.g., tangible) and/or service (e.g., intangible) that's via brick & mortar, online, or a mix thereof, don't hamper your success by presuming your military experiences and credentials are sufficient. A great resource is The Profit television show by Marcus Lemonis.

Launching.

Before you spend money, ensure whether the state you're operating out of provides discounts or exemptions for newly created veteran businesses. Talk to other noncompetitive business owners and supports to identify the exact insurances, policies, coverages, etc., required to protect yourself, loved ones, and the business. For example, although consulting requires little startup cash, it does require professional liability insurance, a company website with analytics, social media platforms and presence, and potentially back office support (e.g., bookkeeping). Ensure you know the costs for your particular venture to mitigate setbacks, financial problems, and marital issues.

Although the failure rate for small businesses within the first year is 20%, 30% second year, and 50% at year 5, what is not mentioned is the workload and money put in to keep the business open until it succeeds or requires the owner to move on. Overall, only 34% of all new businesses make it past 10 years. Thus, you must always pay yourself to secure the livelihood of your loved ones. At the same time, always ensure your pay is reasonable because an inflated salary and a failing business signifies you care more about yourself than the business's success.

Note: A great place to get reasonably priced services for your business needs (e.g., web design, app creation, etc.) is freelancer and fiverr.

Business Canvas.

As with anything, creating the parameters and a distinctive roadmap to success is invaluable. Similar to the five-paragraph operations order, military decision-making process, and course of action brief process, a business canvas enables you to identify: key stakeholders, required actions, minimal resources needed, validated value propositions, supply channels, customer segments, validated cost structure, and viable revenue streams.

In the military, you always compare your current mission, vision, and priorities in relation to your stakeholders (e.g., superiors, peers, subordinates) to ensure your organization is properly aligned with expectations and needs. The business canvas, whether used for self-branding purposes or a small business venture, enables you to align your offering for greater success with the pain you intend to heal with your service and/or product. Therefore, always conduct a business canvas before putting in the time and effort to create a business plan, pitch deck, or elevator pitch.

Business Plan.

When dealing with financial providers such as angel investors, venture capitalists, and financial institutions loans, a business plan is required to demonstrate how well thought out your idea is and their level of risk on return. The plan used to be around 40 pages but is now customarily 10 to 20 pages in length and heavily outlines professionally the items fleshed out during your business canvas process. Often, you can submit your pitch deck in lieu of a business plan. Thus, you should insert a concise and precise narrative for each slide within the notes section so it can stand alone and inform the reader without your presence. As you expand operations, the pitch deck with notes enables new employees to learn about the organization while given a presentation about it.

CHESS STRATEGY

Do you already know what it is you want to do? Are you satisfied continuing your profession in the military? To frame and prioritize the various job opportunities, there is more to consider than desired total compensation (e.g., base, equity, stock, other benefits). For most (unless they were in the private sector at some point before or during their active duty service), determining the right job or opportunity is a journey.

Do you know what industry you would like to work in? Do you want to work for a large corporation, a mid-sized company, or a small startup? Perhaps you have an entrepreneurial bent or passion. How about consulting? How about a full-time opportunity that allows you to do some side consulting while you work on your entrepreneurial pursuit in the background? Whatever your druthers, we recommend that when you make the decision to commit…commit, but be sure to allow yourself enough time to set up you and your family for success with plenty of options.

Don't be like the majority and wait until the last minute to consider your post-military career. Start your job search roadmap at least 18 to 24 months before your final day in the military. As mentioned previously, by starting so far out, you won't have to burn the night oil to ensure you and your loved ones are enjoying the transition versus stressing over it. Knowing early on what your discharge benefits will be (e.g., separation, retirement, disability pay, dental and health care coverages, etc.) enables you to identify the minimum pay you need to sustain your current lifestyle.

Based on the minimum pay you identified to maintain your lifestyle given your benefits and the utilization of cost of living comparison tools, you can identify the proper job(s) for the location(s) sought. Otherwise, you may waste time on misaligned opportunities and undesirable pay ranges. Subsequently, you will enhance your networking efforts because they are more targeted.

Networking.

Networking is by far the most powerful technique in finding unique and exciting opportunities. Remember you must try to get a job that is as high up the ladder as you can instead of settling for less and taking years to get where you should have started. Networking can get you there. The trust created by the network is what will give an employer the necessary comfort to give you the chance in a higher position of authority right out of the military. Otherwise, you are competing against 10 other applicants who have years of experience in the sector and job, whereas you have none. Networking opens doors and enables unsought opportunities. Networking assists in ensuring your first and subsequent post-military jobs are more equitable to your experience and capabilities. In sum, networking can mitigate years of frustration working yourself from the bottom up unnecessarily. Depending on which statistics you use, a job is obtained via networking 60% to 90% of the time.

Yes, networking has a bad taste in the military. Some call it brown nosing, or look at it as a way to gain an advantage over peers for pro-motion (and they aren't wrong about that). The military also looks down on self-promotion, especially in special forces where the term "quiet professional" becomes the code to live by. There is a distinct difference between brown nosing and professionally networking in the military. If you're hesitant to start networking, keep in mind that although silent professionals are preferred, very rarely do they receive what is owed to them because the networker is actively engaging their target, reassessing the battlefield via dialogue, and establishing personal (not professional) mentor/mentee relationships. Relationships and networking are the way of the world, and it is usually an uphill battle competing against those who are networked and have relationships with senior mentors. *It isn't just who you know, it is who they know that is truly powerful.* It is that extension of trust in who we are to those who don't know us; otherwise, it takes too long to establish that trust within the transition timeline.

Speaking of time. Networking takes time. Remember, your success is often equal to how well your reputation proceeds you because your industry experience is frequently significantly less than your competing civilian counterparts. Unfortunately, knowing the importance of networking is half the battle to success. The other half is the time required to invest in effective networking, requiring a person with a planned separation to begin on/about the 18-month mark. Most employers will not consider you an acquirable asset until 90 to 120 days from separation; thus, identifying which industries, type of positions, salaries, benefits, location, etc., beforehand via your network is critical to effectively maximize this remaining window of employment.

You should be conducting first engagements at 18 months out. At this stage, you are just starting to let your existing network know you have decided to retire or leave the service. Know that job announcements are fleeting, making them targets of opportunity. If you are not available and ready, they will get filled and pass you by. Often, you will not have time to focus on jobs until 6 months from separating. Moreover, the latter 6 of the18 months recommended for networking will be heavily bogged down with your military transition process (e.g., Transition Assistance Program briefs, VA disability filing, household goods & transportation coordination, handover of work responsibilities, closeout evaluations, etc.). Thus, having a network in place working on your behalf by the 6-month exit mark benefits in mitigating an income gap.

Take any business cards you have received and put them into your ecosystem, such as their photo, phone numbers, email addresses, and unique details (executive assistant, family interests, etc.). If you engage believing your first and second level of connection will get you the job, your targeting needs realignment. Always assume your ideal job will result from the sixth and seventh levels primarily due to an array of first and second levels speaking highly about you and advocating for you. While coordinating your engagements/touch points, ensure they are frequent enough to be personable and friendship/mentee oriented while mitigating perceptions of being needy, worrisome, or high maintenance. The intent is for them to look forward to your calls, emails, and texts because of the guidance you're seeking from them. Updates should provide shared interests and a personal fellowship sought.

Never fail to send a personal thank you after each engagement to acknowledge their willingness to make time for you and for potential engagements in the future. Think of thank you messages as the military General Officer star note, which only comes from them and is equivalent to bestowing a certificate of appreciation or challenge coin to someone worthy of respect and acknowledgment. You will be amazed how simple acts such as a star note, bringing a bottle of wine to an invitational event, etc., which are common protocol within military senior ranks, enhance your professionalism and character. We know of several service members who got opportunities for writing handwritten thank you notes to senior mentors. It impressed the mentors so much that they reached out to their contacts to get the service members a job.

The extension of trust cannot be overstated enough. For Bill to tell Bob that Heath is a hard worker, mission-focused, and a great family man can't be accomplished by a resume or LinkedIn account alone or combined. The resume or LinkedIn account simply fills in blanks once the extension of trust is established. To have someone vouch for your bona fides is probably the most powerful tool in the job search toolbox. Once again, ensure you start with enough time to let your network frame out.

Executive Coaching.

Executive coaching is invaluable. What is executive coaching? It is usually subject matter experts who advise you on how to better understand yourself and your goals, and will provide you with a framework from which to present yourself to the corporate world.

An executive coach may triangulate your personality with such tests as the Myers-Briggs Personality Type Indicator test. Once you both have identified your personality type, you can have an open dialogue on how to amplify your strengths and shore up your weaknesses when presenting yourself during your job search and most specifically during your interview processes.

Other coaches will pull out your story. This is usually an exercise in describing different past experiences that amplify your skills to achieve quantifiable results. Through their assignments requiring you to develop various stories regarding your past experiences and future goals (e.g., leadership, work experience, biographical), their analysis and critiques permit a self-informed manner of better understanding yourself, the reason for your specific goals, and your baseline for post-military happiness. Once these stories are completed, the next step is usually creating your theme by which you quickly summarize your strengths during an initial job contact. As for cost, some of the transition organizations listed at Appendix C include this service, while others may have to be paid for out of pocket.

Note: The usual personality testing, dialoguing to assess your current psychological state of transitioning (e.g., stressors, goals, issues, etc.) will occur to establish a platform to work from and transform insecurity/unsureness into confident courses of action.

Individual Strengths.

Once you identify the appropriate civilian titles for your military assignments, the next crucial step is identifying one to three things you consistently did at each previous position that enabled you to be successful—your individual strengths.

Your individual strengths are how you are known for operating in a certain manner to succeed. Your reputational strengths are no different from that of Coca-Cola or any other business striving to have something that is similar to, but better than, competitors; meaning, the proprietary manner in which you think, act, and execute in jobs of similar roles and responsibilities as your peers is unique to you. Therefore, where do you constantly succeed (leading, managing, staff work, etc.)? Moreover, what is the ratio between your two lines of success (i.e., 75% leading, 25% staff) and level of autonomy (i.e., 75% empowerment, 25% micro-management).

Interviewing.

When you finally have a face-to-face interview scheduled, remember it resulted from you passing various filtering methods designed to reduce the pool of eligible candidates. Essentially, this means that the position is yours to lose, so don't take it lightly...focus. Also consider the time, money, and resources a company has allocated to your process. Never drink coffee before or during the interview! Coffee loosens lips, and you need to stick to and focus on the specific questions that are asked of you. Don't go down tangents that don't truly relate to the questions, get on a soapbox, or respond with caffeinated enthusiasm. If anything, get a good night's rest and maintain a cool, collected, and thoughtful demeanor.

Informal Interviews. Treat every engagement, whether a phone call, email questionnaire, or discussion, as part of the formal process. Whether the human resources department calls you three times before a formal interview is offered or you receive numerous emails inquiring about additional details, do not take these engagements for granted or let your guard down. In correlation, no matter how relaxed a superior appears or how well you know the people you interact with professionally, you are always being assessed, which will reflect in your interview process. Keep this in mind.

Theme. Even if your competition is like you (e.g., military rank, education, assignments, duty positions, etc.), you must set yourself apart. For example, no two people possess or resolve the same issue identically due to the personalities involved and methods in which actions are undertaken. For example, are you always developing, revamping, innovating, creating... regardless of the organization and duty assignment? One of your key distinguishing factors or reputational strengths is your performance regardless of circumstance. Although some companies provide interview themes in advance, ensure you have three to five themed stories prepared for spur-of-the-moment discussions.

Demonstrate Proficiency. Before you engage, ensure you know both the company and duty description of the job you're seeking. By assessing the company's annual report and other credible public information (e.g., board meeting notes, quarterly reports, strategic plan, etc.), you will be much better prepared for the interview. Moreover, read up on the company's leadership, your specific reporting chain, and those who will interview you. Although many may recommend using LinkedIn to familiarize yourself with others, just remember they will know you have checked them out due to the "who's viewed your profile" feature unless you do so incognito. When performing your research, also utilize Google, NAICS, Facebook, etc., to learn things like the person's professional history, philanthropy efforts, goals/mission/vision, and so on. With the information obtained, it is recommended that you develop 10 to 20 interview questions and how your military experience corresponds to that of the company opportunity. To further refine your proficiency, undergo a murder board interview process (e.g., promotion board preparation) via those you trust to credibly test you.

Military Professionalism. Military professionalism signifies someone with proper behavior and professional qualities. Regardless of the company, network, and interviewer, ensure you speak of your military background in a positive manner to enhance their interest in your unique attributes. In doing so, you mitigate stigmas held by those viewing veterans as "broken heroes" or "entitled," while reinforcing the hard to develop soft skills (e.g., etiquette, communicating, listening, negotiating, etc.) the military is commonly revered for. Also keep in mind that your interviewer may be intimidated because of an inability to relate or from wondering how to lead a military-proven leader (e.g., combat, etc.).

Appearance. You can make a positive impression within seconds of meeting someone. So, to present oneself appropriately is extremely important, especially for the interview process.

Face to Face. For any face-to-face interview, you must be prepared to interview in a business suit…with a tie. Lately the fad is to conduct business in business casual attire (suit with no tie is an example), but for your formal interview a tailored business suit with tie is expected. You should not wear any abnormal colors or bright ties. Instead, wear a neutral but strong navy blue and/or gray suit. Your shirt will be white, and your tie will fit accordingly and not bring attention to it. Your appearance should offer a strong presentation but not one that attempts to outdo your interviewer. Your suit should be tailored; especially for those of you with very athletic builds. The belt matches the shoes, and it doesn't hurt to sport a nice watch. If you believe that you may have a few pounds to lose, plan accordingly and adjust your diet and work out to meet your proposed interview timeline. A shave and new haircut for the men, and fresh makeup and professional hairstyling for the ladies. Plan this no matter the company or interviewer, and you can't go wrong if at the last minute they change the tune (like Amazon) and tell you that a suit is not required but rather jeans and a collared shirt is just fine. Better to be prepared than sorry. Remember if you get to a face-to-face interview, it is your job to win or lose…and every edge helps.

Virtual. The requirement for a virtual interview is no different regarding your professional dress. But now it is time to focus on your background environment. Make sure that your video teleconference background is uncluttered and professional; in fact, a very clean, simple background is desired. Ensure that you are cloistered away from any noise that may intrude on the conversation, and this includes kiddos that may accidentally wander into your home office just wanting to see Dad or Mom. In fact, you may want to conduct this interview outside of the home in a private location. Finally, treat this and every type of interview like it is a face-to-face interview. Never let your guard down and maintain your professional decorum throughout, even if distractions arise. Every single interview is extremely important.

Video Recorded. Once again, make sure your personal appearance is spotless, and that your background environment is uncluttered and clean. You will also need to ensure that your lighting is appropriate for the video camera. Finally, rehearse, rehearse, rehearse. In fact, if you have a spouse or significant other, have them murder board you and critique your responses before you press record. Of note, watch your time! If you don't rehearse your responses multiple times, you can start to ramble and run out of the allotted time. You can imagine how that will look on the receiving end.

<u>Engage Effectively.</u> First impressions are important; they can benefit or hamper your goal regardless of how or where they occur (e.g., phone, email, in-person). It is human nature to measure the worth (perceived) of someone unknown within seconds of engaging. This measuring often occurs first via appearance (e.g., physique, attire, etc.), then interaction (e.g., mannerisms, speech, etc.),

resulting in a personality assumption relative to an operational and cultural fit. Thus, your first impression can be your single point of failure. Although you should put your best foot forward, ensure it is not artificial, because you are also being hired based on fit. Employment timeframes within Corporate America are commonly viewed like those within the military. If you left a job relatively soon, other than for something positive, the questions you may be asked, or your former boss may be asked, may be pointed if the departure resulted from a cultural, organizational, or personality issue. Also, be cognizant that shying away from a response or providing little details to uncomfortable questions can create an alarming climate. As you engage, be attentive without staring.

Humble Confidence. No matter how distinguished your career may be, convey your experiences with *humble confidence* regarding your value proposition. Keep in mind, the value proposition you present will also become part of the metrics by which you are retained. Before you begin initial discussions, ensure you understand the military knowledge level of the person you will be interacting with, to engage at the appropriate level. Forgo the "I'm your best choice" or "Nobody has done what I have" approaches because your competition often will have years of industry experience over you.

Control the Interview. Interviewing is an art form. When done correctly, an interview can subtly transition the interviewer into the interviewee. Near the beginning of the interview inquire about the challenges or problems that need to be solved by you. By doing so, you can better relate how your experiences support their hiring goals. Moreover, you can ask the interviewer how they would solve the problem if they are not your direct supervisor. In the end, each interviewer told you the problem set for you solve and how to solve it and lost sight on interviewing you.

Note: Sometimes interviewing will include testing. Conducting psychological exams online or going so far as to conduct a timed IQ test in the psychologist's office are filtering techniques to see if you are truly right for the job.

SEARCH FIRMS & OTHER OPPORTUNITIES

Search Firms

Search firms are an invaluable asset for you to utilize in the search for your first opportunity out of the military. A search or recruiting firm solicits companies to find the right people for their job requirements. There are a number of search firms out there (you can see a large number of them in *Appendix H*). Some search firms specialize in specific market sectors or focus on certain pay grades such as mid-grade officers and noncommissioned officers. Some search firms are highly reputable at finding the right personnel to fill senior executive ranks and C-Suite (i.e., chief executive officer, chief operations officer, senior vice president) requirements of companies. Regardless, it is highly recommended that you apply to any and all of the recruiting firms that focus on the sector and position you are looking for.

When approaching a search firm, whether an initial phone conversation or face-to-face interview, treat every conversation seriously. Some search firms may try to get you relaxed on purpose to see how you act when your guard is down. Beware of recruiting firms as they work for companies hiring them to find talent. As you work with several firms, ensure that when you accept a job you inform all of the other firms and thank them for their efforts. You may be coming back to them sooner than you think for them to find you that next opportunity, hopefully further up the corporate ladder.

Job Fairs & Hiring Events.

Job fairs, network opportunities, and hiring events are a great place to meet future possible employers, connect and network, and ultimately learn about different sectors. Keep on the lookout for different events that will pop up. Sometimes you may have to travel quite a way to reach them. Network opportunities such as academy events are also great ways to reconnect with old friends who may have been out of the military for a while, and can lead you to the next node in your network or an opportunity itself.

A note to remember: whether physically participating or virtually engaged, ensure that you take advantage of the event to learn more about the companies you are interested in (e.g., operations, structure, benefits, upward progression, etc.) and whether you would professionally and personally fit in well there (e.g., climate, culture, goals, etc.). How you come across is also important at these events. Most people are turned off when you introduce yourself and only talk about what you need, how great you are, and why they need you. On the other hand, people are less guarded when you come to them for more information about their company, where your skills might fit in with their goals, and how their employment process works.

Depending on the type of positions you are looking for, it is highly recommended that you start attending job fairs and hiring events as soon as you commit to the transition. Leave no opportunity unturned to gain insight over your competition.

Note: On-the-spot hiring rarely occurs at job fairs and hiring events because the attendance of hiring managers is not customary.

Online Platforms.

Whenever you apply for a job using LinkedIn, Google, etc., identify employees within the company to reach out to and connect with. The best people to look for are recruiters with a military background, people with military ties, or those who have unique commonalities with you (e.g., education, organizational affiliation, etc.). By doing so, you increase your chances of a response. Whenever you reach out, use messages like, "I applied for a position a while ago and haven't heard anything back, could you be of assistance to ensure I don't owe anything else," "I saw you had a certain position open but am unable to find it, could you be of assistance," or even "I was informed I didn't get selected, are you able to inform me of why so I can increase my chances next time." Refrain from highlighting commonalities with the people you reach out to (i.e., military, schooling, former jobs, etc.). Just as you looked them up, they will most likely do the same in return before responding.

CONCLUSION

The Transition: Preparing for Financial Combat is a state of mind. If you approach each step of this journey with the proper mental state, you will have considerably less stress compared to those waiting until the last minute to begin their transition process. By preparing 18 to

24 months out, you may find the right opportunity; you are well prepared and equipped to step away and seek the next phase in your career. The civilian sector is not a cakewalk; in fact, only the strong and prepared can survive to reach the top. This book was designed to assist you on that journey of managing your expectations, creating coherent roadmaps and frameworks for decision-making, and taking advantage of various education and training opportunities. All of which are essential elements to a successful transition. We hope that the information provided was helpful, and we hope that you find the right opportunity for you and your family in this next phase of your life. Good luck and Godspeed!

APPENDIX A: Service Member Benefits.

eBenefits. Provides access to your official military personnel documents. View the status of your disability compensation claim, transfer entitlement of Post-9/11 GI Bill to eligible dependents (service members only), and register for or update direct deposit information for certain benefits, visit https://www.ebenefits.va.gov/ebenefits/homepage.

Service Records Request. For proving military service (e.g., DD 214/Separation Documents, Personnel Records, Replacement Medals, and/or Medical Records) or to perform genealogical research.

VA Health Care. To apply for VA Health Care benefits as a 10% or more disabled veteran.

Medical Retirement. Intended to compensate for a military career cut short because of disability. If you have less than 20 years of active service, a disability rating of 30% or higher will qualify you for retirement, and a disability rating below 30% will result in separation.

Disability Retirement. For military Reserve technicians separated because of a disability disqualifying them from membership in the military Reserve or holding the military grade required for employment.

Combat Veteran. For service members that served on active duty in a geographical area designated as a combat zone (area of operation). It normally only applies if you engaged directly with the enemy and received fire.

Service-Disabled Veteran. For those who were discharged or released from active duty because of a service-connected disability.

Special Disabled Veteran. For those possessing a serious employment handicap.

MyHealthevet. To refill your VA prescriptions, track delivery, view a list of your VA medications and other details. For tracking your upcoming VA medical appointments, email reminders; communicating securely online with your VA health care team and other VA staff about non-emergency information or questions; entering health information; or to view, print, and download a copy of your VA medical record information.

Education Assistance. For state-level educational benefits available to veterans and their dependents, particularly the children of deceased and disabled veterans.

Colmery Act. On August 17, 2017, Congress signed into law the National Veterans Educational Assistance Act, also known as the Forever GI Bill, to be operated by the US Department of Veterans Affairs. There is also a G.I. Bill comparison tool available for the following benefits:

Post 9/11 G.I. Bill. Chapter 33. Must have served at least 90 aggregate days on active duty after September 10, 2001 or honorably discharged from active duty for a service-connected disability upon serving 30 continuous days. Purple Heart recipients, regardless of length of service, are qualified for Post-9/11 benefits at the 100% level.

Types of Training and Assistance:

1. Correspondence training
2. Cooperative training
3. Entrepreneurship training
4. Flight training
5. Independent and distance learning
6. Institutions of higher learning undergraduate and graduate degrees
7. Licensing and certification reimbursement
8. Vocational/technical training, non-college degree programs
9. National testing reimbursement
10. On-the-job training
11. Tuition assistance top-up
12. Tutorial assistance
13. Vocational/technical training

<u>Montgomery G.I. Bill (MGIB). Chapter 30.</u> Provides education benefits to veterans and service members who have at least 2 years of active duty for college degree and certificate programs, technical or vocational courses, flight training, apprenticeships or on-the-job training, high-tech training, licensing and certification tests, entrepreneurship training, certain entrance examinations, and correspondence courses. Remedial, deficiency, and refresher courses may be approved under certain circumstances. Eligibility is based on four categories:

Category 1. Entered active duty after June 30, 1985 and didn't decline the MGIB in writing upon entry into active duty.

Category 2. Those with remaining entitlement under the Vietnam Era GI Bill (Chapter 34, title 38, US Code).

Category 3. Those who were involuntarily separated for certain reasons or those who were separated under the VSI (Voluntary Separation Incentive) or SSB (Special Separation Benefit) program.

Category 4. Former Veterans Educational Assistance Program (VEAP) participants who elected to convert to MGIB during the open window periods, and for a small group of National Guard.

Montgomery G.I. Bill - Selected Reserve (MGIB-SR). Chapter 1606. Provides education and training benefits to eligible members of the Selected Reserve, including the Army Reserve, Navy Reserve, Air Force Reserve, Marine Corps Reserve and Coast Guard Reserve, and the Army National Guard and the Air National Guard. Assistance covers college degree and certificate programs, co-op training, technical or vocational courses, flight training, apprenticeships or on-the-job training, high-tech training, licensing and certification tests, entrepreneurship training, certain entrance examinations, and correspondence courses. Remedial, deficiency, and refresher courses may be approved under certain circumstances. Eligibility is based on three aspects:

Aspect 1. Must incur a 6-year Selected Reserve obligation. You must enter into a 6-year obligation to serve in the Selected Reserve. If you're an officer, you must agree to serve 6 years in addition to your current obligation.

Aspect 2. Complete your IADT (Initial Active Duty for Training) and Maintain Selected Reserve Status. Serving in a drilling Selected Reserve unit and remaining in good standing.

Aspect 3. Complete High School. You must obtain a high school diploma or equivalency certificate before you apply for benefits.

<u>Reserve Educational Assistance Program (REAP). Chapter 1607.</u> Provides educational assistance to members of the Reserve components called or ordered to active duty in response to a war or national emergency declared by the President or Congress. Eligibility is based on three aspects:

Category 1. Served on active duty on or after September 11, 2001, in support of a contingency operation for 90 consecutive days or more; or

Category 2. Performed full-time National Guard duty under section 502 (f) of title 32 for 90 consecutive days or more when authorized by the President or Secretary of Defense for the purpose of responding to a national emergency declared by the President and supported by Federal funds; or

Category 3. A member called or ordered to active service while serving in the Selected Reserve remains entitled to benefits under REAP only by continuing to serve in the Selected Reserve. A member called or ordered to active service from the Individual Ready Reserve (IRR) remains entitled to benefits under REAP by continuing to serve in the Ready Reserve (either Selected Reserve or IRR).

Vocational Rehabilitation (VOCREHAB). Chapter 31. Assists with job training, employment accommodations, resume development, and job seeking skills coaching. Eligibility is based on two aspects:

Category 1. Active duty service members expecting to receive an honorable or other than dishonorable discharge upon separation from active duty; obtain a memorandum rating of 20% or more from the Department of Veterans Affairs (VA), and apply for VR&E services. Basic period of eligibility ends 12 years from the date of separation from active military service

Category 2. Veterans with a discharge that is other than dishonorable; have a service-connected disability rating of at least 10% from VA; and apply for VR&E services. Basic period of eligibility ends 12 years from the date of notification by the VA of a service-connected disability rating.

Licenses & Certifications. Receive up to $2,000 for a professional skill, minus any fees. There is no limit to the number of tests you may take, or number of times you may take the same test. You may receive reimbursement for approved licensing and certification tests if you qualify for:

(1) Montgomery GI Bill

(2) Montgomery GI Bill Selected Reserves

(3) Reserve Education Assistance Program

(4) Veterans Educational Assistance Program

(5) Dependents Educational Assistance

<u>Yellow Ribbon Program.</u> Provides additional funding to students whose tuition and fees charge exceeds the in-state, under-graduate cap (before August 1, 2011); or charges for out-of-state tuition, or charges in excess of the yearly cap for students enrolled in private institutions (after August 1, 2011). Eligibility is based on three aspects:

Category 1. Served an aggregate period of active duty after September 10, 2001, of at least 36 months and were honor-ably discharged.

Category 2. Were discharged from active duty for a ser-vice-connected disability and you served 30 continuous days after September 10, 2001.

Category 3. Are a dependent who received benefits trans-ferred from an eligible service member.

<u>Apprenticeship & On-The-Job Training.</u> Allows veterans to learn a trade or skill through structured training and close supervi-sion on the job rather than attending formal classroom instruction. Commonly, there is a training contract for a specific period of time with an employer or union resulting in a job certification or jour-neyman status. Eligibility requirements are based on the program availability through both non-Federal and Federal agencies/entities.

<u>Tutorial Assistance (TA).</u> For those receiving VA educational assistance at the half-time or greater rate and have a deficiency in a subject undergone. Pay rate is $100 a month maximum for $1,200 annually. TA is not available to those utilizing the REAP.

Work Study. A Federal minimum wage allowance for full-time or 3/4-time students in a college degree, vocational, or professional program. Veterans with service-connected disabilities of 30% generally receive priority consideration. All duties performed are strictly veteran related.

National Testing Program. Provides reimbursement of all required (mandatory) fees charged (except pre-tests, to receive scores quickly, optional items) for national admission tests, national tests for college credit, and national tests that evaluate prior learning and knowledge and provide an opportunity for credit at an institution of higher learning:

1. SAT (Scholastic Aptitude Test)
2. LSAT (Law School Admission Test)
3. GRE (Graduate Record Exam)
4. GMAT (Graduate Management Admission Test)
5. AP (Advanced Placement Exam)
6. CLEP (College-Level Examination Program)
7. ACT (American College Testing)
8. DAT (Dental Admissions Test)
9. MAT (Miller Analogies Test)
10. MCAT (Medical College Admissions Test)
11. OAT (Optometry Admissions Testing)
12. PCAT (Pharmacy College Admissions Test)
13. TOEFL (Test of English as a Foreign Language)
14. DSST (DANTES Subject Standardized Tests)

15. ECE (Excelsior College Examinations)

16. PLA (Prior Learning Assessment) testing through Learningcounts.org

17. TECEP (Thomas Edison College Examination Program)

Flight Training. For those with a private pilot's license (Rotary wing, B747-400, Dual engine, Flight engineer) and valid medical certification desiring to advance their qualifications.

Entrepreneurship Training. Covers the cost of programs offered by the Small Business Development Center.

Correspondence Training. For those desiring to take lessons in the mail where quizzes and tests are mailed back to obtain grades (not distance learning).

Cooperative Training. For individuals desiring to attend school part-time and work part-time.

Survivors & Dependents Assistance.

Fry Scholarship. For beneficiaries attending school may receive up to 36 months of benefits at the 100% level. Eligibility is based on two aspects:

Category 1. Children under 33 years old of active duty members of the Armed Forces who died in the line of duty after September 10, 2001.

Category 2. Unmarried surviving spouses within 15 years of their active duty spouse's death in the line of duty after September 10, 2001.

Dependents Educational Assistance (DEA). Chapter 35. Benefits may be used for degree and certificate programs, apprenticeship, and on-the-job training. If you are a spouse, you may take a correspondence course. Remedial, deficiency, and refresher courses may be approved under certain circumstances. To qualify, you must be a spouse, son, or daughter (including stepchild or adopted child), of a:

Category 1. Veteran who is permanently and totally disabled as the result of, or dies of, a service-connected disability. The disability must arise out of or be aggravated by active duty.

Category 2. Veteran with a permanent and total service-connected disability who dies from any cause.

Category 3. Service member who is missing in action or is captured in the line of duty and is currently being held by a hostile force.

Category 4. Service member who is currently being forcibly detained or interned in the line of duty by a foreign government or power.

Category 5. Service member who VA determines has a service-connected permanent and total disability; and at the time of VA's determination is a member of the Armed Forces who is hospitalized or receiving outpatient medical care, services, or treatment;

and is likely to be discharged or released from service for this ser-vice-connected disability.

Veterans Educational Assistance Program (VEAP). For those that made educational benefit contributions via military pay of which the government matched contributions on a 2-for-1 basis. Assistance is for college degree and certificate programs, technical or vocational courses, flight training, apprenticeships or on-the-job training, high-tech training, licensing and certification tests, entre-preneurship training, certain entrance examinations, and corre-spondence courses. In certain circumstances, remedial, deficiency, and refresher training may also be available.

Eligibility is based on:

1. Entered service for the first time between January 1, 1977, and June 30, 1985.

2. Opened a contribution account before April 1, 1987.

3. Voluntarily contributed from $25 to $2,700.

4. Completed your first period of service and were discharged or released from service under condi-tions other than dishonorable.

APPENDIX B: Geographic Factors

Arizona. Can subtract up to $2,500 for military pensions in arriving at Arizona taxable income.

Arkansas. Retired military personnel are entitled to a $6,000 exemption.

Colorado. Persons 55–64 years of age as of December 31 may exclude up to $20,000 of their military retirement benefits received during the calendar year. Persons 65 years of age or older, as of December 31, may exclude up to $24,000 of their military retirement benefits received during the calendar year.

Delaware. Individuals under the age of 60 can exclude up to $2,000 of military retirement pay and individuals 60 and over can exclude up to $12,500.

Idaho. Retirement benefits to a retired member of the military 65 or older or disabled and age 62 or older are deductible. The amount deducted must be reduced by retirement benefits paid under the Federal Social Security Act or the Tier 1 Federal Railroad Retirement Act. The maximum amounts that may be deducted are $41,814 for married filing jointly and $27,876 for single. The amount varies from year to year.

Indiana. You can deduct the actual amount of retirement pay received or $5,000, whichever is less, if you meet certain conditions.

Iowa. Up to $10,000 (joint returns), and up to $5,000 (other returns) of military retired pay and SBP benefits may be excluded for those who are 55 years old and older, disabled, and for surviving spouses.

Kentucky. If you retired in 1997 or before, all of your retired military pay is exempt from tax. If you retired after 1997, your pay is subject to state tax if it exceeds $41,110.

Maryland. Military retirees are exempt from Maryland income tax on the first $5,000 of their retirement income. In addition, military retirees who are over the age of 65, totally disabled, or who have a spouse who is totally disabled, receive an additional subtraction.

Missouri. For the tax year beginning January 1, 2012, 45% of a military pension income will be exempt from MO state tax. This tax deduction increased 15% annually until January 1, 2016 when all military pension income became tax free.

Montana. The first $3,600 of retired military pay is exempt from income tax.

New Mexico. The maximum exemption is $2,500. To qualify, the amount on line 7 of the state income tax form must be equal to or less than $36,667 (single), $27,500 (filing married with adjusted gross income less than $51,000 on the joint return), $28,500 for a single taxpayer, or $25,500 for a married taxpayer filing separately.

North Carolina. See the new Bailey decision concerning federal, state, and local retirement benefits.

Oklahoma. Everyone may exclude 75% of their retirement benefits or $10,000 (whichever is greater), but not to exceed the amount included in the federal adjusted gross income.

Oregon. If you receive military retirement pay, you may qualify for a federal pension subtraction. If you are a special-case Oregon resident, your pension remains taxable as Oregon-source income.

South Carolina. Any person retired from the uniformed services with at least 20 years of active duty is allowed an exemption from SC income tax of up to $3,000 until age 65. At age 65 $10,000 of retirement pay is exempt.

Texas. The **Hazelwood Act** provides qualified veterans, spouses, and dependent children with an education benefit of up to 150 hours of tuition exemption, including most fee charges, at public institutions of higher education in Texas. This does NOT include living expenses, books, or supply fees.

Utah. Up to $4,800 of qualified retirement is waived until age 65. At age 65 or older, $7,500 is waived.

West Virginia. An individual, regardless of age, may deduct up to $2,000 of benefits received from military retirement.

Note: This information is subject to sudden changes based on state disposition to military retirement. For instance, to attract military retirees to stay in the state, Maryland has started to address a graduated tax exemption for military pensions.

APPENDIX C: Entrepreneurship

Veterans Business Battle. Rice University in Houston operates this business plan competition to connect veteran-owned companies with growth capital in the form of debt or equity investments. In its first three years, more than $2.5 million of investment offers had been extended to finalists.

Work Vessel for Vets. A nonprofit established to equip America's returning veterans with the tools they need to start a business or pursue career education, such as laptops, tools, equipment, support, etc.

Semper Fi Fund. One of America's highest rated charities, providing urgently needed resources and support for post 9/11 combat wounded, critically ill, and catastrophically injured members of the US Armed Forces and their families via inclusive wellness, education, career, financial, and recreational programs.

Center of Excellence for Veteran Entrepreneurship. A list of national, state, and local resources.

Vetrepreneurship. Lists 100 sites for military veteran businesspeople.

SCORE. A nonprofit partnered with the US Small Business Administration (SBA) providing free business mentoring services to prospective and established small business owners. All volunteers are active or retired business executives and entrepreneurs. SCORE also offers free and low-cost educational workshops via online and in-person.

Small Business Development Center. State and SBA funded to provide free support to entrepreneurs and small businesses. Generally co-located at community colleges, state universities, and/or other entrepreneurial hubs.

Women's Business Center. State and SBA funded to provide free support primarily to women entrepreneurs starting or growing small businesses. WBC seeks to level the playing field against the unique obstacles women still face in the business world.

Goldman Sachs 10,000 Women. A global initiative fostering economic growth by providing women entrepreneurs around the world with a business and management education, mentoring and networking, and access to capital.

Goldman Sachs 10,000 Small Businesses. Provides access to education, capital, and business support services.

APPENDIX D: Transition Programs

HHonors Military Program. By becoming a member, veterans receive a 100,000-point donation to support travel related to job search activities.

FourBlock. A free Career Readiness course offered to current Student Veterans and Active Duty to equip them with the professional development, career exploration, and network needed to make strong career choices and a smooth transition. The FourBlock course has two portions. The online work hosted by Columbia University and then a weekly two-hour class for eight weeks hosted by several of their Corporate Partner at their office location - for industry exposure.

Korn Ferry Leveraging Military Leadership Program. The free program is open to veterans of any rank who left the service in the last two years and service members who will transition in the next 12 months. Participants will be guided by Korn Ferry and Harris global leadership experts, who will lead veterans through a three-month program composed of online, remote, and in-person assessments, coaching, instruction, group exercises, and lectures. Veterans will receive the same research-based leadership development services offered by Korn Ferry to boards, CEOs, and senior executives at leading global organizations.

Education and Employment Initiative (E2I). A Department of Defense (DoD) program that assists wounded, ill, and injured service members early in their recovery process to identify their skills and match them with the education and career opportunities that will help them successfully transition to civilian life

Veterati. The only Veteran Mentorship Platform where you choose successful professional mentors and as many as desired for free one-hour phone calls.

American Corporate Partners (ACP). A national nonprofit organization focused on helping returning veterans find their next careers through one-on-one mentoring, networking, and online career advice. ACP's Citizens Mentoring Program encourages individuals not affiliated with one of ACP's Partner Companies to become ACP Mentors. ACP's Women's Veteran Mentoring Program launched in 2016 and connects female veterans with female entrepreneurs and business leaders for yearlong mentorships. Women veterans have access to exclusive networking events and career development workshops. ACP AdvisorNet is an online career Q&A community designed to assist an increasing number of veterans and current service members with networking and career advice.

COMMIT Foundation. High-impact, tailored workshops and one-on-one transition assistance programs for top veteran talent that educate veterans on the value of their knowledge, skills, and abilities.

The Station Foundation. Special Operators Only.

Your Grateful Nation. Special Operators Only.

Hires Heroes USA. Provides free career coaching and job sourcing to hundreds of transitioning US military members, veterans, and military spouses each week.

Deloitte Core Leadership Program. Helps veterans and armed forces members (1) define their personal brand, identify their strengths, and be able tell their own story; (2) learn innovative networking strategies and communication techniques, which include best practices in using social media, through personalized and repetitive employment simulations; (3) interact and network, from the start of the program, with Deloitte leaders as well as professionals from the public and private sectors; and (4) gain access to other alumni of the CORE Leadership Program.

Hiring our Heroes – Corporate Fellowship Program. Provides transitioning service members with management training and hands-on experience in the civilian workforce, expanding Corporate America's understanding of the veteran job market and preparing those individuals for smooth transitions into meaningful civilian careers. In select locations, the program is extended to military spouses and veterans.

APPENDIX E: Training & Education

Joint Service Transcript. An academically accepted document approved by the American Council on Education (ACE) to validate a service member's military occupational experience and training along with the corresponding ACE college credit recommendations. It provides a description of military schooling and work history in civilian language. It serves as a counseling tool for academic and career counselors in advising service members and veterans. It serves as an aid in preparing resumes and explaining military work experience to civilian employers. It also saves time and money by awarding academic credits, which means less tuition to pay and less time spent in the classroom.

Warrior-Scholar Project. Provides free one to two-week courses focused on mentoring and other forms of guidance for enlisted service members wishing to attend four-year universities at four-year universities. The program seeks to teach the skills required for effective and successful learning in the college environment.

Pro-Learn. Provides 30-days free project management professional training online for service members, veterans, and their family members. Full services have a 40% discounted rate which includes the exam fee, PMI membership fees, PMBOK, 1-year access to all of our training and resources including one on one coaching, and if you fail, they pay for the re-test.

Institute for Veterans & Military Families. Delivers free class-leading programs in career, vocational, and entrepreneurship education and training, providing service members, veterans, and their families with the skills needed to be successful in education, work, and life. The program consists of two career preparation & employment, eight entrepreneurships & small business, and two community support programs.

Vets2PM. Provides a project management professional certification process that meets the project development units required and translates military experience into required project management hours for testing.

MSys Training. Provides veteran discount training and professional certification in Project Management, Lean Six Sigma, Information Technology, etc. Note: Lean Six Sigma testing is open book with three testing attempts unlike other programs, which are closed book and one attempt.

Troops to Teachers. Helps you begin a new career as a public-school teacher — giving you the opportunity to use your leadership skills, knowledge, and experience to have a positive effect on our nation's youth. The program provides counseling and referral services for participants to help them meet education and licensing requirements to teach. Subsequently, the program helps them secure a teaching position.

Veterans Entrepreneurial Jumpstart (VEJ) Program. Designed specifically to provide the tools, education, and mentorship necessary to allow all qualified veterans the opportunity to start their own businesses. The course is available at multiple universities, and the cost is free if selected.

National Forum for Black Public Administrators. The principal and most progressive organization dedicated to the advancement of black public leadership in local and state governments. The *NFBPA* is an independent, nonpartisan, nonprofit organization founded in 1983. Its Executive Leadership Institute (ELI) is dedicated to grooming African American managers for the rigors of executive positions in public service organizations.

Founder Institute. An American business incubator, entrepreneur training and startup launch program. It offers a four-month part-time program for new and early-stage entrepreneurs that helps them develop their business ideas and form a company. Among the key requirements for graduation is the creation of a fully operational company by the end of the four-month program.

Bunker Labs. A national not-for-profit organization built by military veteran entrepreneurs to empower other military veterans as leaders in innovation. It supports military veterans throughout the journey of starting a business: from the idea stage—where active duty service members are thinking about what to do post-service—to the growth stage of successful companies looking to hire, raise capital, and expand into new markets.

Hack Reactor. A 12-week full-time or part-time software engineering Coding Bootcamp education program. Prior industry or academic experience is not required.

National Veterans Entrepreneurship Program (VEP). Provides a rigorous entrepreneurial learning and development opportunity for veterans with service-connected disabilities and those who have uniquely distinguished themselves in the military. The VEP is designed for veterans interested in starting a new venture as a means to financial independence and for veterans who have an existing business for which they would like to increase profits. The course is available at multiple universities, and the cost is free if selected.

Galvanize. Cultivates tech talent for both companies and individuals with courses in full-stack web development and data science via full-time, part-time, and online programs.

Hire Our Heroes Cybersecurity. Free training and certification preparation courses for veterans.

EH Academy. Provides a free cybersecurity and hacking course among other free and fee-based courses.

Credentialing Opportunities On-Line (COOL). Helps service members identify certifications and licenses relating to work experiences. It also explains how to obtain these civilian certifications, and their license requirements, including links for numerous resources to get started.

College Level Examination Program (CLEP). Service members can earn introductory college-level credit for what they already know on 33 different examinations for over 2,900 higher education institutions at over 1,800 test centers. DoD paid courses automatically populate on the Joint Services Transcript; however, exams paid out-of-pocket must be submitted for inclusion.

DANTES Subject Standardized Tests (DSST). Nationally recognized program offering college credits for learning acquired outside a traditional classroom for subject areas like Social Sciences, Math, Applied Technology, Business, Physical Sciences, and Humanities via 30-plus exams.

Air Force Virtual Education Center. Provides a wide array of online services empowering education to include the creation and management of online tuition assistance.

Marine Corps Voluntary Education Center. Provides a variety of free educational services to active duty military, family members, civilian employees, and reservists.

Naval Education & Training Professional Development Center (NCVEC). Provides information to select an appropriate education path, degree plan, and school; educational counseling; pre-college and entrance exams; and available funding sources.

Army Continuing Education Division (ACED). Provides soldiers, family members, and civilians services and information on education and career counseling; testing, assessment, and evaluation services; leadership development; tuition assistance; career management; and transition assistance.

Education & Training Quota Management Command. An organization tasked with providing education for active duty members, officers, reservists, auxiliarists, and Coast Guard civil employees.

TA DECIDE. An information and comparison tool designed specifically to aid participants of DoD's tuition assistance program in making informed choices on schools and education programs.

Servicemembers Opportunity College Career & Technical Education Program (SOC CTE). A list developed to assist military education counselors, academic advisors, and military members with identifying career and technical education pathways to civilian careers with positive growth potential.

Military Spouse and Family Educational Assistance Programs. This program is a partnership between the US Department of Education and US Department of Veterans Affairs (VA) to make it easier for disabled veterans to have federal student loans discharged. The US Department of Education will match borrowers on the National Student Loan Data System that possess loans or aid via the Teacher Education Assistance for College and Higher Education Grant Program.

Tutor.com. For service members and their dependents to receive free live-tutoring and homework support online.

APPENDIX F: Interviewing

Appearance. Don't let the first time you've worn a tie, dress shoes/heels, tailored pants/suit, button-up/button-down shirt, etc., be during the interview. Being comfortable in your "dress to impress" attire is as important as having it to wear. Moreover, know when it's appropriate to wear a shirt with cufflinks, that button-down shirts (buttons on the collar) require a tie, wide-collar shirts are best with bowties and ties with large knots, and cuffed slacks are best with heeled dress shoes. Additionally, pay attention to the color and design of your nails, jewelry, clothing, and associated logos regarding the nonverbal messages they may send based on the climate and culture of the organization and persons you are interacting with. The internet has a wealth of information to guide you on appropriate choices for attire for an interview.

STAR Method. A 90–120 second structured way of holistically responding to a question by presenting your *situation*, identifying your *task*, highlighting your *action*, and concluding with the tangible *result*.

Behavioral Questions. A method for employers to have you recount past experiences so that they may assess future performances. The following are a few examples to prepare for:

a.   Tell me a time you worked effectively under pressure.

b.   Describe a time you made a mistake and how did you handle it.

c.   Give an example of a goal you set and how you went about to reach it.

    d.   Describe an unpopular decision you made and how you managed your team.

Face to Face. Dress to impress based on the climate and culture of the organization interviewing you. A rule of thumb is to wear neutral but professionally strong colors (i.e., grey, blue, black, white, etc.). Ensure you color-coordinate both your outfit and accessories (i.e., belt, watch, jewelry, socks, shoes, undershirt, etc.). As needed, ensure you look physically healthy and fit, because being visually acceptable (i.e., haircut, edged, shaved, trimmed, reasonable amount of makeup, etc.) is a nonverbal discriminator.

Note: Similar to how you judge your leaders, peers, and subordinates based on first encounters regardless of reviewing their military credentials previous to an introduction, you establish assumptions on how people may fit within an organization's climate, and your level of personal engagement with them, before they even speak, based on their visual acceptability.

Virtual. Your appearance is of the utmost importance as you do not have the opportunity to interact in a way that a face-to-face setting enables. Unlike a face-to-face interview, you have a responsibility to ensure your background, lighting, and level of noise intrusion are optimally favorable. Similar to a face-to-face engagement, never allow yourself to become complacent. Just because you have the liberty of conducting your interview in a familiar and comfortable environment, don't let nonverbal cues contradict your verbal ones.

Note: Always plan for Murphy's Law; always mitigate potential embarrassments (i.e., family interruption, construction work, other work responsibilities).

Video Recorded. Ensure you select a space where the background and lighting are complementary to your nonverbal goals in association with the climate and culture or the organization you're interviewing with. To mitigate rambling, long, and complex responses, or going over your allotted time, craft a few questions with tailored responses to rehearse. Before conducting your live-recorded responses, ensure you quickly review your notes so your attention and focus is at the camera and not on your notes.

Note: Always look at the camera, otherwise your recorded response will have you looking distracted or as if you are talking to someone else.

APPENDIX G: Internships & Cooperative Education (Co-Op)

Textron. Internships and co-ops offered for engineering, supply chain & operations, finance, accounting, information technology, human resources, development, communications, government affairs, program management, and legal.

Vertiv. Focused on business, technology, and innovation skills development via an undergraduate summer paid internship or six-month co-op.

Hendrickson. For individuals interested in working with the world's leading supplier of truck, tractor and trailer suspensions; auxiliary lift axle systems; steel leaf springs, and metal bumpers for the heavy-duty transportation industry.

HillVets House Fellowship. A community of Veterans, Service-members, and their supporters interested in governance, international affairs, policy and politics. We strive to open doors for our members and to provide them with contacts, education, and resources to continue positive career progression.

The Washington Center. Provides a diverse selection of world-class internship programs and seminars in the heart of Washington, D.C., for free.

Turner Bridge Program. A summer undergraduate program for those interested in construction.

TJX. A merchandising development co-op lasting six months as an allocation analyst or associate buyer. The allocation analyst analyzes and discovers trends to plan exactly how much product goes in stores. The associate buyer chooses the right product and therefore travels with buyers and meets with vendors to determine the products customers will want to buy.

Turner Construction Company. A summer internship for undergraduates pursuing engineering, construction management, safety, architectural studies, finance, accounting, or human resources.

Edward Jones. A 14-week (20 hours a week) paid operations co-op for business, finance, and accounting majors.

American Airlines. A technical operations co-op for those interested in aerospace, avionics, electrical and mechanical engineering within fleet or power plant engineering.

Comcast. Internships and co-ops for undergraduates in various positions. Internships are 11 weeks and co-ops are six months.

Disney Careers. Heroes Work Here is an initiative to hire, train, and support veterans in multiple areas.

Lockheed Martin. Internships and co-ops for engineering mathematics, physics, business, finance, supply chain, human resources, and associated disciplines.

Central Intelligence Agency. Undergraduate full-time paid internships in various positions.

Defense Intelligence Agency Internship. An internship for undergraduate or graduate students pursuing foreign area studies, computer science, business administration, human resources, public administration, international relations, legal, political science, chemistry, physics, biology, microbiology, pharmacology, toxicology, engineering, or intelligence analysis. Pay is generally GS-5 to GS-9.

Vets2Cloud. A co-op apprenticeship program helping veterans enter the workforce as salesforce business consultants. Over the course of two to three years, we mentor and coach veterans in three distinctive areas to help with their transitions in the areas of business structure, salesforce consulting, and wellness.

Department of Labor. Provides apprenticeships spanning more than 1,000 occupations including careers in health care, cybersecurity, information technology, and energy.

APPENDIX H: Search Firms

Heidrick & Struggles. A global executive search firm that also possesses a consulting practice focused on leadership and culture shaping.

Korn Ferry. An executive search and recruiting firm known for its headhunting technology. Services range from executive recruitment to leadership development programs, enterprise learning, succession planning, and recruitment outsourcing; to include surveys of its clients and other employers regarding trends in hiring. It also possesses a human resources global management consultancy and Futurestep. com, which is utilized to help candidates at middle management find positions to advance their careers.

Egon Zehnder. A global executive search that is the world's third largest. It also provides Board Consulting and Leadership Strategy Services.

Spencer Stuart. A privately owned American global executive search and leadership consulting firm. The *Wall Street Journal* described Spencer Stuart as the US government's main resource for finding replacement executives for companies bailed out.

Lucas Group. North America's premier executive recruiting firm for mid-tier to Fortune 500 clients ranging from mid-level to senior positions.

Bradley-Morris. The leading military recruiting firm specializing in transitioning military and veteran talent. We make the translation between military skill sets and civilian talent profiles for top leadership, technical, sales and operations career opportunities with Fortune 1000 employers.

Cameron-Brooks. Guides junior military officers through every step of their military transition process to start their business career.

Sterling Group. A veteran-owned executive search firm specializing in executive-level opportunities for industry-altering talent within manufacturing, consumer products, transportation & logistics, financial services, health care, retail, information technology, aerospace, and energy.

Orion Talent. Provides a full-cycle military talent program that address all phases of the process, from sourcing, candidate attraction and recruiting, through on-boarding, integration, and retention.

Stewart, Cooper & Coon. Specializes in placing six-figure executive candidates from all industries and fields both in the United States and abroad.

Reffett Associates. A small veteran-owned executive boutique firm for those with extensive experience in retail and consumer packaged goods, private equity, commercial & federal services, government sectors and associations and non-profits.

Alliance Careers. Junior military officer recruiting firm with a cap of 300 accepted per year.

Development Resources Inc. A nonprofit executive search firm.

USA Jobs. The United States Government's official website for listing civil service job opportunities.

CSI Executive Search. A nationwide Forbes Top 20 executive recruiting firm specializing in operational and technical placements in major metro locations.

Workforce Agency. The governor of each state designates the administration of Wagner-Peyser Act funded employment and workforce information services, and the state's unemployment compensation program. Each agency helps in finding a job, getting job search help, locating local workforce services, and accessing career information.

State Veterans Affairs Offices. Helps veterans file claims for education, locate health care, find employment, get a veteran home loan, and offers more services to those who are entitled.

US Army Civilian Human Resources Agency (USACHRA). Provides employment assistance to retirees, veterans, their family members and federal employees affected by reduction in force (RIF) and base realignment and closure (BRAC).

Department of the Navy (DON) Civilian Human Resources. Prior to applying on USAJOBS, you can identify DON organizations and respective senior executive service members.

APPENDIX I: Online Job Hunting

LinkedIn. Mainly used for professional networking, including employers posting jobs and job seekers posting their CVs.

ZipRecruiter. Provides job boards and tools for applicant tracking and screening. Focuses on small businesses that may not have the brand to attract a lot of candidates.

Ladders. Lists only vetted job offers with annual salaries of $100,000 or more. Full access requires an annual fee.

Monster.com. Helps those seeking work to find job openings, for lower to mid-level employment, that match their skills and location.

Indeed. Services include job search, recommended job, job trends, resume upload, storage and search, industry trends, salary search, job competition index, and website forums.

ChronicleVitae. Presents news, information, and jobs for college and university faculty and student affairs professionals (staff members and administrators).

Chronicle of Philanthropy. Presents news, information, and jobs for the nonprofit world.

APPENDIX J: Veteran Programs

Bank of America's Veteran's Associate Program (VAP). A unique 10-week rotational program for recently transitioning veterans. The program includes training and development, access to senior leaders, networking, market compensation, and the opportunity to be considered for full-time employment at the conclusion of the program.

Bank of America's Global Technology & Operations Military Development Program. Gives veteran leaders the opportunity to successfully leverage military experience and skills in our corporate environment. The program is designed to give associates the necessary tools to further manage their professional development, realize their future potential, and maximize their contributions to Bank of America.

USAA VetsLeaD. A 12-month program that develops and retains newly hired and recently separated veteran employees hired into various professional and staff level roles at USAA. Participation in VetsLeaD helps to close the business acumen gap many veterans have when leaving military service.

JP Morgan Chase Military Officers Executive Development Program (MOEDP). Designed to identify top junior military officers and develop them into future business executives within the operations functions of consumer and community banking. Three one-year rotations across consumer and community banking operations occur as a project manager, analyst, and team leader while working in marketing, risk, lending, and fraud operations.

JP Morgan Chase Military Pathways Development Program (MPDP). A highly selective program that seeks to identify top veteran talent and provide candidates the training, opportunities, and exposure they need to grow into future leaders within operations, technology, risk & controls, strategy, or cybersecurity. During a 24-month period individual rotation occurs every 12 months into project manager, analyst, and people leader while working in marketing, consumer risk, digital technology, analytics, and operations. Upon completion, placement into full-time roles based on preference, performance, and growth potential occur.

Sherwin Williams Global Supply Chain High Velocity Leadership Program (HVLP). For those desiring a leadership role in distribution. The 9 to12 month job shadowing is with distribution service center operations managers to learn day-to-day warehouse and fleet operations, to include safety, quality, service, people, and cost.

General Electric Junior Officer Leadership Program (JOLP). A unique opportunity to work in three different functions, in eight-month rotations with one of the following businesses: aviation, health care, power & renewables, transportation, and Baker Hughes, a GE Company. Qualified, exceptional candidates are selected to start their civilian careers in this two-year, cross-functional, rotational training program, which includes both on-the-job and formal classroom training.

Accenture Junior Military Officer Program (JMOP). Designed for transitioning leaders with supply chain, procurement, human resources, marketing, technology, operations, or project management & leadership experience.

Kaiser Permanente JMOP. A two-year rotational program offering work in information technology, enterprise shared services, national facilities services, human resources, care management institute, or health care administration. The program includes on-the-job experiences, leadership mentoring, and formal web-based and classroom training.

Amazon Military Leadership Program. For innovative, talented, and experienced leaders seeking to become highly influential senior leaders and executives within critical business areas.

Citigroup Military Officer Leadership Program (MOLP). A transitional leadership development program. The MOLP utilizes customized development paths to developing skills in financial services management. Associates in the MOLP participate in three targeted experiential learning opportunities through work assignments over a 24-month period, classroom-based learning opportunities, active coaching and mentoring with assigned senior leaders and business partners, project engagements, and peer support initiatives.

CoreLogic Leadership Program (LeaP). For transitioning junior military officers with operations, logistics, and leadership experience. The LeaP is an accelerated leadership development composed of three rotations to learn business foundational operations, quality and process improvement, and management-level placement upon completion.

Hiring Our Heroes Corporate Fellowship Program. Provides transitioning service members management training and hands-on experience within the civilian workforce. In select locations, military spouses and veterans can participate.

Vocational Rehabilitation & Employment (VR&E). A Department of Veterans Affairs (Chapter 31) and Statewide Workforce Commission program providing service-connected disability veterans assistance via five (5) tracks: previous employer reemployment, employment rapid access, self-employment, long-term services, and independent living services. Additionally, most states have their own VOCREHAB programs a veteran can concurrently utilize.

APPENDIX K: Claiming Disability

Disabled American Veterans (DAV). Chartered by the United States Congress for disabled military veterans of the United States Armed Forces to help them and their families through various free services like pre-discharge claims assistance, Veteran Benefits Administration guidance, and outreach programs.

American Legion. Chartered and incorporated by Congress in 1919 as a nonprofit patriotic veterans organization devoted to mutual helpfulness. Services include centers for benefits, career, education, health, and financial assistance. It is also known for drafting and passing the G.I. Bill and for its political lobbying of benefits such as pensions and the Veterans Health Administration.

Military Order of the Purple Heart. Congressionally chartered and exclusively for those with a purple heart. Its service program assists with filing claims for benefits.

Paralyzed Veterans of America. Congressionally chartered to support those with spinal cord injury or dysfunction. It provides holistic recovery and transition for severely disabled veterans through integrative programs and services, with services also offered to able-bodied, ill, wounded, and injured veterans as well as their dependents, survivors, and caregivers, free of charge.

Veterans of Foreign Wars. Organized for those that honorably served in wars, campaigns, and expeditions on foreign soil or hostile waters to speed their rehabilitation and assist their widows, orphans, and dependents.

American Veterans (AMVETS). Federally chartered and the oldest veteran support organization that advocates legislatively for improvements in health care and benefits that affect all veterans, those currently serving, and their families.

APPENDIX L: Bio-Resume

LARRY WALLACE JR., Ph.D.

University of Texas System

Leadership Development & Veterans Affairs

210 W. 7th Street, Austin TX 78701

Office of Academic Affairs

Larry is the Director of Veterans Support & Leadership Programs at the University of Texas System Administration and President of Wallace Brothers & Associates which provides small business strategic planning. Prior to UTS, Larry served as Executive in Residence for VETTED, a nonprofit veterans transition program, upon retiring from the US Army.

Larry earned his doctorates from Northcentral University, is a University of Texas at Arlington Alumni, holds an MBA and master in human relations & business, executive leadership certificates in entrepreneurship by Texas A&M - Commerce & Saint Joseph University, a Business Skills Certificate from the University of Pennsylvania at Wharton, a selectee to attend the National Defense University's Joint Special Operations Masters of Arts in Strategic Studies, and a 2018 Dissertation of the Year Nominee. He is also Lean Six Sigma – Green Belt certified & project management trained.

Larry is a retired combat veteran that served as Chief of Staff to the Chief People Officer and Deputy Chief of Staff for the U.S. Army Special Operations Aviation Command (Airborne) during the integration of women into combat roles; Chief of Staff to the Chief of Intelligence & Operations and a Managing Director for USA NATO during the "Don't Ask, Don't Tell Repeal Act of 2010, European base closures, and realignment of NATO forces; Director of People for an Infantry Task Force overseeing Anbar Province, the largest in Iraq; a Top Tier US Postal Managing Director supporting Southern Iraq; ROTC Recruiter for the University of Texas at Arlington, Managing Director of a Drill Sergeant Training Company over the Mid-Cities; Drill Sergeant at Fort Sill, Oklahoma; and the Department of the Army Promotion System & Customer Service Senior Manager for the 25th Infantry Division & Johnston Island.

Within nonprofit, Larry served as Greek Life President over 25+ organizations, National Pan-Hellenic Council Community Services Director; Alpha Phi Alpha Fraternity, Inc., Graduate Advisor, and Mascot at the University of Texas at Arlington. He also served as President for 3 districts & 13 local bodies; a State Junior Vice President; Strategic Director for 4 states; Chief Administrative Officer for 3 national staffs; an Adjunct Professor for Central Texas College; a College Proctor for 3 universities; and an Assistant Scoutmaster. Larry served as a radio personality for Blackberry Gospel Radio and Vice Chairman & Strategic Planning Chair for C2 Change (mental health support to youth and their families). He currently serves as an Employment & Training Advisory Member for Texas Veterans Commission; Veterans Advisor to the Travis County Commissioner - Precinct 1; National Association of Healthcare Senior Executives member; Ambassador to the Travis County Healthcare Division (Central Health); and Councilman and former Planning & Zoning Commissioner at City of Manor (7th fastest growing suburb in America - realtor.com, 2018). Larry is also co-author of The Transition: Preparing for Financial Combat which spearheaded the U.S. Army Sergeants Major Academy's transition elective revision.

Recognitions bestowed are 2019 Austin 40 Under 40 Finalist for Youth & Education then Civics, Government, and Public Affairs; 42 performance awards; 2 district staff member of the year awards; a community service & president of the year award; 3 honorary & 25 invitational memberships; and induction into the Golden International Honour Society, Delta Mu Delta International Honor Society in Business, and the International Scholar Laureate Program for Business & Entrepreneurship program.

Larry is married to the former Jamilah Sharp of Atlanta, Georgia, and father of Levi, and twins Madison and Elijah.

HEATH J. NIEMI

Street Address

City, State Zip Code

Phone:

Email:

Colonel Heath Niemi is a 1992 West Point Graduate and veteran of 20 combat tours in Afghanistan and Iraq with the 160th Special Operations Aviation Regiment. Colonel Niemi is transitioning out of the military and the U.S. Army Special Operations Aviation Command (USASOAC) after 25 years of service in the spring of 2017.

Heath is currently the Chief of Staff for the commanding general of the USASOAC and in charge of a staff of 144 personnel and 22 sub-divisions (the CFO, COO, CIO, HR, acquisition, legal and medical directors report to him) that resources and trains special operation aviation to support the most elite special operations ground forces around the globe. As the portfolio director for the enterprise, Heath oversees the $750 million annual budget and the $3.9 billion Future Years Defense Program (FYDEP) for an organization composed of 4200 personnel and 204 aircraft which include specially modified helicopters, fixed wing, and unmanned systems worth in excess of $6.1 billion.

An inspirational leader, Heath is a driver of organizational change. He created the organization's knowledge management system for daily operations and programs that led to savings in time, money, and increased cross functional awareness. Additionally, he led a human resource transformation of the organization to fix manpower authorizations and streamline responsibility. On a side note, he initiated an analysis of the flying hour algorithm which led to a $130-million-dollar savings in the FYDEP.

Other unique capabilities Heath possesses is the ability to virtually lead a globally dispersed organization as he led a team (Battalion) that was employed across Iraq, Afghanistan, Asia and the U.S. simultaneously. He was also involved in the initial deployments to both Afghanistan in 2001 and Iraq in 2003, where he participated in the evolution of systems and processes to include global command and control and logistics. In combat, he was the Commander of all Joint Task Force Special Operation Army Aviation assets in theater on twelve separate deployments.

With 25 years of leadership and management experience, Heath has a masters of leadership and management as well as a masters of strategic studies from the U.S. Army War College where he studied macro geopolitical government and military strategy and was recognized as a distinguished graduate.

Other interesting notes. Heath was the only World Helicopter Team Gold Medalist for the U.S. team in 1996 and once a nationally ranked power lifter in the U.S.P.F. He created and writes a daily investment blog called Strategic Stimulus that correlates macroeconomics for day trading. He is also currently writing academic works on future methods of warfare to include autonomous drones and is working with U.S. Army War College on the future of technologically enabled leadership.

He is married to the former Michele Holmes of Nashville, Tennessee and is the proud father of two daughters, Kimber 4 and Kendall 3.

APPENDIX M: Cover Letter

Name

Street Address

City, State, Zip Code

Phone, Email

To Whom It May Concern,

Thank you for taking time out of your busy day to review my resume. I am very excited to be considered for the position. I would like to contribute my 18-plus years of experience in the Department of Defense and various nonprofit organizations to the success of your company.

Throughout my career, I have gained strong expertise in the areas of continual improvement (Lean Six Sigma & project management) and cognition (strategic planning & agile leadership). Through my attention to detail, I consistently improved efficiencies and productivity by over 20% within the various entities I worked for.

Furthermore, my interpersonal skills, both written and verbal, enable levels of confidence and long-lasting relationships amongst stakeholders suitable for innovative customer support and operations.

Sincerely,

Your Name Here

APPENDIX N: Executive Resume

LARIMEN 'LARRY' WALLACE II

Mailing Address
Phone Number
Email Address
https://www.linkedin.com/in/larrywallacejr

PROFESSIONAL SUMMARY

Seeking opportunities to serve near Austin, Texas, within Education, Healthcare, Philanthropy, or Politics. I possess 18+ years of corporate stewardship interacting and collaborating with multiple levels of management and diverse cultural audiences within complex high-tempo environments. I consistently increased workforce productivity by 20% through long-term action-oriented plans that effectively streamlined process, enhanced efficiency, and strengthened brand recognition.

SKILLS / ATTRIBUTES

- Change Management
- Human Capital Development
- Project / Lean Management
- Diversity / Inclusion
- Strategizing / Best Business Practices
- HR / Operational Metrics

CERTIFICATIONS / MEMBERSHIPS

- Lean Six Sigma - Green Belt
- Project Management Training (Syracuse University)
- Small Business Operations (Texas A&M University)
- Business Plan & Venture Pitching (St. Joseph University)
- Business Skills Foundations (University of Pennsylvania)
- Innovation & Leadership (University of Texas at Austin)
- American College of Healthcare Executives
- National Association of Healthcare Services Executives
- Golden Key International Honour Society
- Delta Mu Delta International Honor Society in Business

EDUCATION

Doctor of Philosophy: Business Administration, Northcentral University
Master of Business Administration: Management, Northcentral University
Master of Science: Human Relations and Business, Amberton University
Bachelor of Arts: Organizational Leadership, University of Texas at Arlington
Associate of Arts: General Studies, Central Texas College

PROFESSIONAL EXPERIENCE

Director of Veterans Affairs & Leadership Programs (2018 - Present)
University of Texas System - Fortune 100 Equivalent
                                                        Austin, Texas

- Ranked #1 in Texas & Nation's 2nd largest system with 8 academic & 6 health science campuses, 216K students, 100K employees, and $24B endowment issuing 1/3rd (undergraduate) & 2/3rd (healthcare) of Texas' degrees. Top 10 most innovative system.
- Collaborated with Organizational Effectiveness, Academic & Health Affairs, Research, Faculty & Student Advisory Councils enhancing the climate & culture of veteran support 50% by realigning and identifying program needs & resources required.
- Served as veteran lead to government agencies, veteran service organization, nonprofit and corporate entities at the City, State, and National levels increasing collaboration & productivity by 50%
- Led the 10th Annual "All-State" Texas Veterans Higher Education Symposium, and UT Veterans Symposium enhancing services & support via increased collaboration by 50%

Deputy Chief of Staff (2015 - 2017)
U.S. Army Special Operations Aviation Command (Airborne) - Fortune 100 Equivalent
                                                        Fort Bragg, North Carolina

- Increased operational capacities & strategic planning by 50% for a 4K employee (soft assets $2B+), $6.1B capital, and $750M budgeted 1-star enterprise comprising 22 departments dispersed across multiple locations servicing the Nation's most elite forces
- Regained 10K+ labor hours annually by streamlining processes as the Chief of Administration, Strategic Communications, Protocol; including Executive Officer Representative to the U.S. Army Special Operations Command (3-star Fortune 100 equivalent)
- Managed 30+ Industry, DoD & Partner Nation engagements; revised regulations, implemented human capital programs, and collaborated support efforts with the U.S. Special Operations Command (4-star) & U.S. Joint Special Operations Command (3-star)

Chief of Staff to the Chief People Officer (2013 - 2015)
U.S. Army Special Operations Aviation Command (Airborne) - Fortune 100 Equivalent

Fort Bragg, North Carolina

- Led a team of 10 (soft assets $4.5M+), directly supporting 144 employees & 4K indirectly that doubled HR strategic planning & operations for an 'all things aviation' resourcing enterprise for the U.S. Army Special Operations Command
- As the initial test unit, developed a tracking system capturing recruitment, training, assignment selection, and acclimation processes for Congress' female combat exclusion repeal initiative
- Managed critical & essential recruitment, requisition, and evaluation reports between the U.S. Army Recruiting Command (2-star, Fortune 100), U.S. Army Special Operations Command, U.S. Joint Special Operations Command, and Department of the Army
- Orchestrated a Secretary of the Army approved statue, 5+ Army Chief of Staff approved memorials, and 10+ Department of the Army annual recognitions worth $300K+ in soft assets; and improved employee satisfaction 30% via incentive & retention revisions

Managing Director (2010 - 2013)
Bravo Company, Allied Forces North Battalion (NATO) - Fortune 100 Equivalent   **Heidelberg, Germany**

- Led a $400K+ capital, 120 employee company (soft assets $66.6M+) spanning 2 countries at 6 locations managing U.S. manpower to NATO Allied Forces Air & Land Commands (4 & 3-star Fortune 100's) & Center of Excellences (Czech, Ingolstadt, France, Slovakia)
- Orchestrated with U.S. European Command (4-star); Eurocorp, U.S. Army Europe & U.S. Embassies (3-stars), and Joint Center of Excellences the 1st U.S. person with family to the Czech Republic, and the future placement 7 at France & 3 at Slovakia
- Led footprint maneuvering collaborations to mitigate support gaps for a NATO Allied Forces Air Command expansion, Land Command & multiple Garrison closures, while undergoing transfer of resources and company closure concurrently
- Increased relations with 20+ partner nation 50% & regained 40K+ labor hours annually via revised resourcing processes, operating transparently, rebranding, and establishing an effective mission, task list, and human capital development process

Chief of Staff to the Chief of Intelligence / Operations Officer (2010)
U.S. Army, NATO - Fortune 100 Equivalent   **Schweinfurt, Germany**

- Led a team of 5 (soft assets $2M+) within a 2-star enterprise overseeing antiterrorism & force protection measures for 3K+ employees with families in 12 countries at 34 locations
- Coordinated a senior executive leader's summit for 20+ U.S. general officers (1 to 3-star), senior executive service members (equivalent), Ambassadors (equivalent), and executive leaders to address & resolve quality of life issues and challenges
- Regained 200K in misused resources & enhanced the role, mission, and organizational structure via a strategic planning conference

U.S. Army / U.S. Army Reserves (1999 - 2010) - Fortune 500 / 1000 Equivalent   Hawaii, Texas, Germany
Platoon Leader (Managing Director - Iraq) / Drill Sergeant Training Commander (Managing Director) / Drill Sergeant (Instructor) / U.S. Army - Hawaii Customer Services Noncommissioned Officer in Charge (Senior Manager) / U.S. Army - Hawaii Centralized Promotions Board N.C.O.I.C. (Senior Manager) / U.S. Army - Hawaii Evaluations & Records Specialist / Battalion Personnel Officer (Director of People - Iraq)

ADDITIONAL EXPERIENCE

Nonprofit, Educational, and Recognitions   Europe, Maryland, North Carolina, Texas
- City Councilman; Employment & Training Advisory Member for Texas Veterans Commission; Higher Education Chair for Texas Military Spouse Economic Empowerment Zone (San Antonio); Chair for University of Texas' Veterans Leadership Task Force; Veterans Advisor for Travis County Commissioner Court - Precinct 1; Co-Author of The Transition: Preparing for Financial Combat
- Former Nonprofit Special Advisor to CEO of Grateful Heart - Comprehensive Veteran Services (counseling & referrals) & Former Executive in Residence for VETTED and its pilot program of 25 Veterans in partnership with UT-Austin & UPENN Wharton
- Nonprofit Vice Chairman for C2 Change (mental illness support) & Former Radio Personality for Blackberry Gospel Radio; revised 5-district and 2-national protocol manuals; developed 2 state educational programs
- President for 3 districts and 13 local bodies, a state Junior Vice President, Strategic Director for 4 states, Chief Administrative Officer for 3 national staffs, and bestowed 3 honorary and 25 invitational memberships
- International Scholar Laureate Program (Business & Entrepreneurship) recipient; Community Health Champion (Ambassador) for Travis County Healthcare Division (Central Health); 2018 Dissertation of the Year Nominee
- Adjunct Professor and Proctor for the University at Maryland University College and Central Texas College
- 2019 Austin 40 Under 40 Finalist, 27 performance / proficiency, 5 foreign relations, 3 teamwork, 3 cultural diversity, 2 adversity / courage, 2 personifications, 2 district staff members of the year, 1 community service, and 1 president of the year award
- Member of Society of Human Resource Management, Dallas Human Resource Management Association, Entrepreneurship) recipient, Association of the United States Army member, and National Defense University Joint Special Operations Masters of Art's in Strategic Studies Selectee

HEATH J. NIEMI

Street Address	Phone:
City, State Zip Code	Email:

Executive Summary

Combat-proven Special Operations Army officer & aviator transitioning to an aerospace and defense technology company. With executive experience directing complex operations in high pressure settings, will bring thoughtful execution to an organization and leadership team. Possesses excellent communication and interpersonal skills resulting in partnerships that foster a collaborative atmosphere. Successfully led an organization with a fiscal operating budget in excess of $750 million for operational programs and capital inventory in excess of $6.1 billion.

Core Competencies

- Strategy Development
- DOD Relationships
- Create Empowered Environments
- Cultural Change

- Top Secret/SCI Clearance
- Program Management
- Operations & Logistics Planning
- Capital Investment

- Executive Leadership
- Decision Making
- International Operations

Professional Experience

President/Chief of Staff (Colonel)
US Army Special Operations Aviation Command (USASOAC), Fort Bragg, NC   2015 – Present

- Transformational executive leader with oversight for an annual $750+ million budget and a $3.9 billion Future Years Defense Program (FYDP) who facilitated the development of the USASOAC 2035 Future Strategy and Vision.
- As the Air Staff Chief of Staff of the U.S. Army Special Operations Command (USASOC), directly coordinated with the Special Operations Command (SOCOM), the Department of the Army (DA) at the Pentagon, Geographic Combatant Commands (GCC), Theater Special Operations Commands (TSOC), the Army Aviation Center of Excellence (USAACE) and Industry.
- A portfolio director who streamlined the Strategic Planning Process to more effectively nest operations, procurement, research and development in the Program Objectives Memorandum (POM) for FY 19-23 and FY 20-24, resulting in successfully completing the organization's programs and projects in a fiscally constrained environment.
- Oversight of the USASOC Unmanned Aviation System (UAS) program to include Group IV, Group III, and Group II UAS. Established the UAS operational planning team that created the USASOC UAS Group III Capability Development Document (CDD) for the next generation Group III system. Directly coordinated with SOCOM to bring the CDD to SOCREB (Special Operations Command Requirements Evaluation Board).
- Facilitated the establishment of the USASOC ISR council. Responsibility for the integration of intelligence, surveillance, and reconnaissance capability on assigned unmanned aerial systems and systems within the USASOC enterprise.
- Created the Army Special Operations Command 'Synthetic Readiness' Concept with a focus on virtual, augmented and mixed reality to fill the gap of network distributed systems within Special Operations Command with oversight from the Services and the Joint Staff. Led the initiative to fund a RAND study to analyze the ability of the Army to network to Special Operations distributed systems to enable collective training.
- Led the USASOAC Operational Planning Team for the next generation Future Vertical Lift rotary wing program as the USASOAC was the lead for SOCOM and was also completely integrated with DA for planning.

Senior Vice President of Operation/G3, Deputy Chief of Staff – Operations
US Army Special Operations Aviation Command, Fort Bragg, NC, Various Global Locations   2012 – 2014

- Driven leader responsible for solving organizational capability gaps to include building partner nation special operations aviation capabilities, enhanced unmanned aviation systems, and modular, flexible joint special operations aviation command structures. Started the initiative that led to the USASOC Group III replacement initiative and ensuing CDD. Proponent for advanced ISR sensors integration on UAS systems.

121

- Led, managed, and coached 51 highly trained professionals creating a high-performance team of teams to ensure 22 subdivisions were provided with the best equipment, training, and manpower.

Battalion Commander, Pilot-in-Command
4/160th Special Operations Aviation Regiment (Airborne), JBLM, WA; Iraq, Afghanistan, Asia   2010 – 2012

- Led a globally distributed special operations aviation unit comprised of 580 personnel and 26 highly modified aircraft that conducted air combat and training operations with multiple U.S Government agencies, foreign nationals, and other military services in Iraq, Afghanistan, and Asia resulting in tactical success with strategic impact in support of the Department of Defense.
- Developed the 160th SOAR's vision for networked, distributed systems. This initiative led to successfully integrating a Battalion simulation requirement into the FY 15-19 Program Objectives Memorandum (POM).

Regiment Executive Officer
US Army, 160th Special Operations Aviation Regiment (Airborne), Fort Campbell, KY   2009 – 2010

- Led transformational change and procurement of specialized equipment to smoothly transition the organization to a more flexible, agile, and powerful force
- Lead director of the executive staff members ensuring they function proactively in supporting 2,347 personnel who operated and maintained 174 aircraft to support national missions.

Vice President of Operations/Regiment S3 – Operations
US Army, 160th Special Operations Aviation Regiment (Airborne), Fort Campbell, KY   2008 – 2009

- Led, planned, resourced, and synchronized training and combat operations, organizational transformation, and force modernization requirements for an organization with 2,437 personnel, and 400 federal employees.
- Facilitated the creation of the first USASOAC Gray Eagle units that included intimate coordination with SOCOM, USASOC, and DA.

Director of Operations/Battalion S3 – Operations
US Army, 1/160th Special Operations Aviation Regiment (Airborne), Fort Campbell, KY   2006 – 2008

- As a Combat Task Force Commander, remained calm, focused, and flexible in chaotic, hostile environments.

Various Leadership Roles, Domestic and Abroad   1992 – 2008

- Hand-selected for the elite 160th Special Operations Aviation Regiment (Airborne) during a competitive process; served from 2000 - 2012 with this premier unit in Afghanistan and Iraq.
- Various jobs including Company Commander, Company Executive Officer, Special Mission Unit Liaison Officer.

Education

- MSS, Strategic Studies (Distinguished Graduate), US Army War College, Carlisle, PA, 2015
- MA, Leadership and Management (Summa Cum Laude), Webster University, Webster Groves, MO, 2006
- BS, Engineering Management, US Military Academy, West Point, NY, 1992

Certification

- PMP, Project Management Professional

Additional Information

Author.

- "The Trouble with Mission Command, Flexive Command and the Future of Command Control", *Joint Forces Quarterly*
- "My Droneski Just Ate Your Ethics", War on the Rocks
- "Synthetic Readiness: The Remedy for Future Joint Readiness", War Room U.S. Army War College

Military Awards and Decorations.

- The Legion of Merit, Combat Action Badge, four Bronze Stars and eight Air Medals to include one with Valor device.

YOUR NAME
Insert Duty Description

City, State
Contact Number
Hyperlinked Email

PROFILE

Insert info here...

CORE COMPETENCIES

-
-
-
-
-

-
-
-
-
-

CAREER HIGHLIGHTS

-
-
-
-

PROFESSIONAL EXPERIENCE

Title, Department | Organization
Location. | XXXX – Present
Organization overview (up to four lines) ...
- Single or two-line bullets (three to five bullets per organization) ...
-
-
-

EARLIER PROFESSIONAL EXPERIENCE

Title, Department | Organization, Location | XXXX-XXXX
Up to four lines in paragraph format to highlight experience past 10 years that support the resume's focus...

HONORS AND AWARDS

Title, Organization, XXXX; **Name**, XXXX, ...

PROFESSIONAL AFFILIATIONS

- **Representative to the Military Coalition, Army Aviation Association of America (AAAA), 2017 – Present**
Author monthly articles, for AAAA Magazine, on congressional issues regarding Army Aviation.
- **Advisory Board Member, Dean's Advisory Board, University of Central Florida College of Engineering, 2016 – Present**
Periodic guest lecturer for engineering management courses in an industrial engineering graduate program.

EDUCATION AND PROFESSIONAL DEVELOPMENT

- **Type of Degree**, University Name, Department, XXXX
- **Certificate Name, Level / Number**, Granting Authority, XXXX

123

APPENDIX O: General Schedule (GS) Equivalent Civilian to Military Ranks

Civilian Grade	Military Rank	Army Title
GS-1	E-1	Private
GS-2	E-2	Private 2
GS-3	E-3	Private First Class
GS-4, GS-5	E-4	Specialist, Corporal
GS-6	E-5	Sergeant
GS-6, GS-7	E-6	Staff Sergeant
GS-7	E-7	Sergeant First Class
GS-7	E-8	Master Sergeant or First Sergeant
GS-7	E-9	Sergeant Major or Command Sergeant Major
GS-8	W-1	Warrant Officer 1
GS-8	W-2	Chief Warrant Officer 2
GS-8	W-3	Chief Warrant Officer 3
GS-8	W-4	Chief Warrant Officer 4
GS-8	W-5	Master Warrant Officer
GS-9	O-1	Second Lieutenant
GS-10	O-2	First Lieutenant
GS-11, GS-12	O-3	Captain
GS-13	O-4	Major
GS-14	O-5	Lieutenant Colonel
GS-15	O-6	Colonel
SES Level V	O-7	Brigadier General
SES Level IV	O-8	Major General
SES Level III	O-9	Lieutenant General
SES Level I & Level II	O-10	Army General

APPENDIX P: General Schedule (GS) Required Waiting Periods

The required waiting periods established by law for advancement to the next higher step as a GS employee are as follows:

Advancement from...	Requires...
step 1 to step 2	52 weeks of creditable service in step 1
step 2 to step 3	52 weeks of creditable service in step 2
step 3 to step 4	52 weeks of creditable service in step 3
step 4 to step 5	104 weeks of creditable service in step 4
step 5 to step 6	104 weeks of creditable service in step 5
step 6 to step 7	104 weeks of creditable service in step 6
step 7 to step 8	156 weeks of creditable service in step 7
step 8 to step 9	156 weeks of creditable service in step 8
step 9 to step 10	156 weeks of creditable service in step 9

The GS pay scale can be found here to include salaries with and without the additional locality stipend, https://www.federalpay.org/gs/2017.

APPENDIX Q: Senior Executive Service (SES)

Generally, the SES is comprised of high-level officials who are above the GS-15 level of the General Schedule (GS) pay scale.

These pay levels represent guidelines for agencies to use for setting the salaries of their top officials. Minimum pay under the ES scale is set at 120% of the basic pay for a GS-15 Step 1 employee, while the maximum compensation that can be paid to an ES employee is the current salary of the Vice President of the United States.

Level Description	Minimum	Maximum
Agencies with Certified SES Performance Appraisal System	$126,148	$189,600
Agencies without Certified SES Performance Appraisal System	$126,148	$174,500

ES Level	Education Level	Salary
ES Level 1	Ph.D.	$210,700
ES Level 2	Ph.D.	$189,600
ES Level 3	Ph.D.	$174,500
ES Level 4	Ph.D.	$164,200
ES Level 5	Ph.D.	$153,800

APPENDIX R: Blended Retirement System

The blended retirement system (BRS) was established for all new service members with an effective date of January 1, 2018. It also possessed an opt-in option for those with less than 12 years of service and 4,320 retirement points until December 31, 2018. To learn more on what your blended retirement stipend will be, access the DoD Approved BRS Calculator.

Note: The BRS calculator does not incorporate legacy thrift savings plan contributions or savings bonds purchases under the former (legacy) retirement plan.

The following info is an excerpt from the Frequently Asked Questions Regarding the New Blended Retirement System file from the Department of Defense, dated May 1, 2017.

All service members joining on or after January 2018 are automatically enrolled into a thrift savings plan (TSP) at a 3% contribution based on their basic pay; to which, the Department of Defense (DoD) will contribute 1% of that same basic pay automatically after 60 days in service and will vest at years based on the pay entry base date (PEBD). At two (2) years in service, the DoD will match contributions at 4% with a maximum of 5%. However, upon the 26th year of service DoD contributions cease.

Unlike the legacy retirement system's 2.5% multiplier, the blended system calculates retired pay with a 2% multiplier and the highest 36-months of basic pay. If you choose to receive 25% or 50% lump sum of the discounted present value of future retirement payments, your monthly retired pay will be reduced until you are eligible for full social security retirement age (usual age 67).

Lump-sum elections must occur at least 90 days before retirement. Although the money received is not recouped in the event of death, the remaining annuity will terminate unless you are enrolled in the survivor benefit plan.

Note: The lump sum is considered earned income and is therefore taxable. Thus, you may elect to receive your lump sum in up to four (4) installments over a four (4) year period to reduce the tax burden.

Member's TSP Contributions	DoD Automatic 1% into TSP	DoD Matching TSP Up to 4%
After 60 days	After 60 days	After 2 years

You Contribute	DoD Auto Contribution	DoD Matches	Total
0%	1%	0%	1%
1%	1%	1%	2%
2%	1%	2%	5%
3%	1%	3%	7%
4%	1%	3.5%	8.5%
5%	1%	4%	10%

APPENDIX S: Legacy Retirement System

There are four plans under the legacy retirement system, which are *Final Pay, High 36 Month Average, Special Computation for Career Status Bonus with Reduced Retirement (CSB/REDUX)*, and *Disability* that pay monthly based on a percentage multiplier of 2.5% per year of service to base pay. To decide which method below applies to you, you must determine your date of initial entry to military service (DIEMS) or date of initial entry to uniformed services (DIEUS). It is a fixed date that does not change regardless of how many times you may have reentered into the military.

Retirement Plan	Basis	Multiplier	COLA	Readjustment	Bonus
Final Pay	Final basic pay	2.5% per year	CPI	None	None
High-36	Average of highest 36 months of basic pay	2.5% per year	CPI	None	None
CBS/REDUX	Average of highest 36 months of basic pay	Same as High-36 with reduction of one percentage point for each year short of 30 years of service	CPI - 1%	At age 62, 1) retired pay made equal to High-36 2) future multiplier made equal to High-36 3) future COLA continues at CPR - 1%	$30,000 at 15th year of service with obligation to serve 20 year career
Disability	Either Final Pay or High-36 as appropriate	2.5% per year of % of disability member's choice	CPI	None	None

The *CSB/REDUX* pay only applies to active duty members and reduces the *High 36* multiplier by 1% for each year less than 30 years served. *Disability* pay is generally what provides a greater payment than the *High 36* multiplier and the disability percentage assigned at retirement.

Note: 75% is the cap for disability retirement.

Years of Service	10	15	20	21	22	23	24	25	30	35	40	41
Final Pay	25%	37.5%	50%	52.5%	55%	57.5%	60%	62.5%	75%	87.5%	100%	102.5%
High-36	25%	37.5%	50%	52.5%	55%	57.5%	60%	62.5%	75%	87.5%	100%	102.5%
REDUX*	N/A	N/A	40%	43.5%	47%	50.5%	54%	57.5%	75%	87.5%	100%	102.5%

REDUCTION FACTORS APPLICABLE TO TEMPORARY EARLY RETIREMENT AUTHORITY					
Months Less than 240	Reduction Factor	Months Less than 240	Reduction Factor	Months Less than 240	Reduction Factor
1	.99917	2	.99833	3	.99750
4	.99667	5	.99583	6	.99500
7	.99417	8	.99333	9	.99250
10	.99167	11	.99083	12	.99000
13	.98917	14	.98833	15	.98750
16	.98667	17	.98583	18	.98500
19	.98417	20	.98333	21	.98250
22	.98167	23	.98083	24	.98000
25	.97917	26	.97833	27	.97750
28	.97667	29	.97583	30	.97500
31	.97417	32	.97333	33	.97250
34	.97167	35	.97083	36	.97000
37	.96917	38	.96833	39	.96750
40	.96667	41	.96583	42	.96500
43	.96417	44	.96333	45	.96250
46	.96167	47	.96083	48	.96000
49	.95917	50	.95833	51	.95750
52	.95667	53	.95583	54	.95500
55	.95417	56	.95333	57	.95250
58	.95167	59	.95083	60	.95000

The following TERA Computations are per the Defense Finance & Accounting Service.

RPB   -   Retired Pay Base (i.e. high 36 monthly average basic pay)
AS   -   Active Service (in months)
MO   -   Months in a year
RPF   -   Retired Pay Percentage Factor
TRF   -   TERA Reduction Factor (Table 3-5)

$$RPB \times ((AS \div MO) \times RPF) \times TRF =$$
$$\$3{,}783.50 \times ((187 \div 12) \times .025) \times .95667 =$$
$$\$3{,}783.50 \times (15.5833 \times .025) \times .95667 =$$
$$\$3{,}783.50 \times .3896 \times .95667 =$$
$$\underline{\$1{,}410.18}$$

RPB   -   Retired Pay Base
360   -   30-Years (360-months)
AS   -   Active Service (in months)
MO   -   Months in a year
RPF   -   Retired Pay Percentage Factor
RRF   -   REDUX Reduction Factor (1%)
TRF   -   TERA Reduction Factor (Table 3-5)

$$RPB \times ((AS \div MO) \times RPF) - (((360 - AS) \div MO) \times RRF)) \times TRF =$$
$$\$3{,}783.50 \times ((187 \div 12) \times .025) - (((360 - 187) \div 12) \times .01)) \times .95667 =$$
$$\$3{,}783.50 \times ((15.5833 \times .025) - ((173 \div 12) \times .01)) \times .95667 =$$
$$\$3{,}783.50 \times (.3896 - (14.42 \times .01)) \times .95667 =$$
$$\$3{,}783.50 \times (.3896 - .1442) \times .95667 =$$
$$\$3{,}783.50 \times .2454 \times .95667 =$$
$$\underline{\$888.24}$$

If you took the CSB/REDUX, you may be subject to additional penalties if TERA eligible. Per the Finance Management Policy, Military Pay Policy for Retired Pay, the following is the current retired pay chart:

Years	Months	(%)	Years	Months	(%)	Years	Months	(%)	Years	Months	(%)
		00.	3		7.50	6		15.00	9		22.50
	1	00.20	3	1	7.70	6	1	15.20	9	1	22.70
	2	00.43	3	2	7.93	6	2	15.43	9	2	22.93
	3	00.63	3	3	8.13	6	3	15.63	9	3	23.13
	4	00.83	3	4	8.33	6	4	15.83	9	4	23.33
	5	1.05	3	5	8.55	6	5	16.05	9	5	23.55
	6	1.25	3	6	8.75	6	6	16.25	9	6	23.75
	7	1.45	3	7	8.95	6	7	16.45	9	7	23.95
	8	1.68	3	8	9.18	6	8	16.68	9	8	24.18
	9	1.88	3	9	9.38	6	9	16.88	9	9	24.38
	10	2.08	3	10	9.58	6	10	17.08	9	10	24.58
	11	2.30	3	11	9.80	6	11	17.30	9	11	24.80
1		2.50	4		10.00	7		17.50	10		25.00
1	1	2.70	4	1	10.20	7	1	17.70	10	1	25.20
1	2	2.93	4	2	10.43	7	2	17.93	10	2	25.43
1	3	3.13	4	3	10.63	7	3	18.13	10	3	25.63
1	4	3.33	4	4	10.83	7	4	18.33	10	4	25.83
1	5	3.55	4	5	11.05	7	5	18.55	10	5	26.05
1	6	3.75	4	6	11.25	7	6	18.75	10	6	26.25
1	7	3.95	4	7	11.45	7	7	18.95	10	7	26.45
1	8	4.18	4	8	11.68	7	8	19.18	10	8	26.68
1	9	4.38	4	9	11.88	7	9	19.38	10	9	26.88
1	10	4.58	4	10	12.08	7	10	19.58	10	10	27.08
1	11	4.80	4	11	12.30	7	11	19.80	10	11	27.30
2		5.00	5		12.50	8		20.00	11		27.50
2	1	5.20	5	1	12.70	8	1	20.20	11	1	27.70
2	2	5.43	5	2	12.93	8	2	20.43	11	2	27.93
2	3	5.63	5	3	13.13	8	3	20.63	11	3	28.13
2	4	5.83	5	4	13.33	8	4	20.83	11	4	28.33
2	5	6.05	5	5	13.55	8	5	21.05	11	5	28.55
2	6	6.25	5	6	13.75	8	6	21.25	11	6	28.75
2	7	6.45	5	7	13.95	8	7	21.45	11	7	28.95
2	8	6.68	5	8	14.18	8	8	21.68	11	8	29.18
2	9	6.88	5	9	14.38	8	9	21.88	11	9	29.38
2	10	7.08	5	10	14.58	8	10	22.08	11	10	29.58
2	11	7.30	5	11	14.80	8	11	22.30	11	11	29.80

Years	Months	(%)	Years	Months	(%)	Years	Months	(%)	Years	Months	(%)
12		30.00	15		37.50	18		45.00	21		52.50
12	1	30.20	15	1	37.70	18	1	45.20	21	1	52.70
12	2	30.43	15	2	37.93	18	2	45.43	21	2	52.93
12	3	30.63	15	3	38.13	18	3	45.63	21	3	53.13
12	4	30.83	15	4	38.33	18	4	45.83	21	4	53.33
12	5	31.05	15	5	38.55	18	5	46.05	21	5	53.55
12	6	31.25	15	6	38.75	18	6	46.25	21	6	53.75
12	7	31.45	15	7	38.95	18	7	46.45	21	7	53.95
12	8	31.68	15	8	39.18	18	8	46.68	21	8	54.18
12	9	31.88	15	9	39.38	18	9	46.88	21	9	54.38
12	10	32.08	15	10	39.58	18	10	47.08	21	10	54.58
12	11	32.30	15	11	39.80	18	11	47.30	21	11	54.80
13		32.50	16		40.00	19		47.50	22		55.00
13	1	32.70	16	1	40.20	19	1	47.70	22	1	55.20
13	2	32.93	16	2	40.43	19	2	47.93	22	2	55.43
13	3	33.13	16	3	40.63	19	3	48.13	22	3	55.63
13	4	33.33	16	4	40.83	19	4	48.33	22	4	55.83
13	5	33.55	16	5	41.05	19	5	48.55	22	5	56.05
13	6	33.75	16	6	41.25	19	6	48.75	22	6	56.25
13	7	33.95	16	7	41.45	19	7	48.95	22	7	56.45
13	8	34.18	16	8	41.68	19	8	49.18	22	8	56.68
13	9	34.38	16	9	41.88	19	9	49.38	22	9	56.88
13	10	34.58	16	10	42.08	19	10	49.58	22	10	57.08
13	11	34.80	16	11	42.30	19	11	49.80	22	11	57.30
14		35.00	17		42.50	20		50.00	23		57.50
14	1	35.20	17	1	42.70	20	1	50.20	23	1	57.70
14	2	35.43	17	2	42.93	20	2	50.43	23	2	57.93
14	3	35.63	17	3	43.13	20	3	50.63	23	3	58.13
14	4	35.83	17	4	43.33	20	4	50.83	23	4	58.33
14	5	36.05	17	5	43.55	20	5	51.05	23	5	58.55
14	6	36.25	17	6	43.75	20	6	51.25	23	6	58.75
14	7	36.45	17	7	43.95	20	7	51.45	23	7	58.95
14	8	36.68	17	8	44.18	20	8	51.68	23	8	59.18
14	9	36.88	17	9	44.38	20	9	51.88	23	9	59.38
14	10	37.08	17	10	44.58	20	10	52.08	23	10	59.58
14	11	37.30	17	11	44.80	20	11	52.30	23	11	59.80

Years	Months	(%)	Years	Months	(%)	Years	Months	(%)	Years	Months	(%)
24		60.00	27		67.50	30		75.00	33		82.50
24	1	60.20	27	1	67.70	30	1	75.20	33	1	82.70
24	2	60.43	27	2	67.93	30	2	75.43	33	2	82.93
24	3	60.63	27	3	68.13	30	3	75.63	33	3	83.13
24	4	60.83	27	4	68.33	30	4	75.83	33	4	83.33
24	5	61.05	27	5	68.55	30	5	76.05	33	5	83.55
24	6	61.25	27	6	68.75	30	6	76.25	33	6	83.75
24	7	61.45	27	7	68.95	30	7	76.45	33	7	83.95
24	8	61.68	27	8	69.18	30	8	76.68	33	8	84.18
24	9	61.88	27	9	69.38	30	9	76.88	33	9	84.38
24	10	62.08	27	10	69.58	30	10	77.08	33	10	84.58
24	11	62.30	27	11	69.80	30	11	77.30	33	11	84.80
25		62.50	28		70.00	31		77.50	34		85.00
25	1	62.70	28	1	70.20	31	1	77.70	34	1	85.20
25	2	62.93	28	2	70.43	31	2	77.93	34	2	85.43
25	3	63.13	28	3	70.63	31	3	78.13	34	3	85.63
25	4	63.33	28	4	70.83	31	4	78.33	34	4	85.83
25	5	63.55	28	5	71.05	31	5	78.55	34	5	86.05
25	6	63.75	28	6	71.25	31	6	78.75	34	6	86.25
25	7	63.95	28	7	71.45	31	7	78.95	34	7	86.45
25	8	64.18	28	8	71.68	31	8	79.18	34	8	86.68
25	9	64.38	28	9	71.88	31	9	79.38	34	9	86.88
25	10	64.58	28	10	72.08	31	10	79.58	34	10	87.08
25	11	64.80	28	11	72.30	31	11	79.80	34	11	87.30
26		65.00	28		72.50	32		80.00	35		87.50
26	1	65.20	29	1	72.70	32	1	80.20	35	1	87.70
26	2	65.43	29	2	72.93	32	2	80.43	35	2	87.93
26	3	65.63	29	3	73.13	32	3	80.63	35	3	88.13
26	4	65.83	29	4	73.33	32	4	80.83	35	4	88.33
26	5	66.05	29	5	73.55	32	5	81.05	35	5	88.55
26	6	66.25	29	6	73.75	32	6	81.25	35	6	88.75
26	7	66.45	29	7	73.95	32	7	81.45	35	7	88.95
26	8	66.68	29	8	74.18	32	8	81.68	35	8	89.18
26	9	66.88	29	9	74.38	32	9	81.88	35	9	89.38
26	10	67.08	29	10	74.58	32	10	82.08	35	10	89.58
26	11	67.30	29	11	74.80	32	11	82.30	35	11	89.80

Years	Months	(%)	Years	Months	(%)	Years	Months	(%)	Years	Months	(%)
36		90.00	38		95.00	40		100.00	42		105.00
36	1	90.20	38	1	95.20	40	1	100.20	42	1	105.20
36	2	90.43	38	2	95.43	40	2	100.43	42	2	105.43
36	3	90.63	38	3	95.63	40	3	100.63	42	3	105.63
36	4	90.83	38	4	95.83	40	4	100.83	42	4	105.83
36	5	91.05	38	5	96.05	40	5	101.05	42	5	106.05
36	6	91.25	38	6	96.25	40	6	101.25	42	6	106.25
36	7	91.45	38	7	96.45	40	7	101.45	42	7	106.45
36	8	91.68	38	8	96.68	40	8	101.68	42	8	106.68
36	9	91.88	38	9	96.88	40	9	101.88	42	9	106.88
36	10	92.08	38	10	97.08	40	10	102.08	42	10	107.08
36	11	92.30	38	11	97.30	40	11	102.30	42	11	107.30
37		92.50	39		97.50	41		102.50	43		107.50
37	1	92.70	39	1	97.70	41	1	102.70	43	1	107.70
37	2	92.93	39	2	97.93	41	2	102.93	43	2	107.93
37	3	93.13	39	3	98.13	41	3	103.13	43	3	108.13
37	4	93.33	39	4	98.33	41	4	103.33	43	4	108.33
37	5	93.55	39	5	98.55	41	5	103.55	43	5	108.55
37	6	93.75	39	6	98.75	41	6	103.75	43	6	108.75
37	7	93.95	39	7	98.95	41	7	103.95	43	7	108.95
37	8	94.18	39	8	99.18	41	8	104.18	43	8	109.18
37	9	94.38	39	9	99.38	41	9	104.38	43	9	109.38
37	10	94.58	39	10	99.58	41	10	104.58	43	10	109.58
37	11	94.80	39	11	99.80	41	11	104.80	43	11	109.80

ABOUT THE AUTHORS

Hon. Larry Wallace Jr., Ph.D.
Captain, U.S. Army (Retired)

Larry is the Director of Veterans Support & Leadership Programs at the University of Texas System Administration, President of Wallace Brothers & Associates, and former Executive in Residence for VETTED.

Larry is a combat veteran with multi-industry experience. In the military, he served in various leadership roles for Personnel Services Battalions, Initial Entry Training Centers, an Infantry Task Force, ROTC, USA NATO, and Special Operations. Within nonprofit, Larry served as President for 3 districts & 13 local bodies; a State Junior Vice President; Strategic Director for 4 states; and Chief Administrative Officer for 3 national staffs. Within academia, he served as an Adjunct Professor, College Proctor, Greek Life President, National Pan-Hellenic Council Community Services Director; Graduate Advisor, and University Mascot. In 2019, Larry was recognized as an Austin 40 Under 40 Finalist (Youth & Education Category).

Post military, Larry served as a radio personality for Blackberry Gospel Radio; former Vice Chairman & Strategic Planning Chair for C2 Change (mental health support to youth and their families); Employment & Training Advisory Committee Member for Texas Veterans Commission; Veterans Advisor to the Travis County Commissioner Court - Precinct 1; National Association of Healthcare Senior Executives member; Ambassador to Travis County Healthcare Division (Central Health), Councilman and former Planning & Zoning Commissioner at City of Manor (7th fastest growing suburb in America - realtor.com, 2018); and Co-Author of The Transition: Preparing for Financial Combat

Heath J. Niemi
Colonel, U.S. Army (Retired)

Colonel (Retired) Heath Niemi is Vice President of Global Sales & Development at Martin UAV. In this capacity, Heath is responsible for establishing global business development with emphasis on the U.S. Army and Special Operations Command. He is also responsible for capture and project management activities to include business-to-business research and development for the company while introducing the new V-BAT, 'equipment independent' VTOL UAS to global markets. Heath is a 1992 West Point Graduate and combat veteran of 20 combat tours in Afghanistan and Iraq with the 160th Special Operations Aviation Regiment (Airborne). Heath previously served as Chief of Staff for the U.S. Army Special Operations Aviation Command (Airborne), commanded and served in executive positions within the 160th Special Operations Aviation Command (Airborne). Of interest, Heath was also the only World Helicopter Team Gold Medalist for the U.S. team in 1996 and a past U.S.P.F. nationally ranked power lifter. Heath is also known for his daily investment blog called Strategic Stimulus which correlates macroeconomics for day trading. He also writes academic works on future methods of warfare to include a published work on the future of technologically enabled leadership called 'Flexive Command'.